Grammar for High School

A Sentence-Composing Approach—
A Student Worktext

There is a kind of carpentry in sentence making, various ways of joining or hooking up modifying units [that is, sentence-composing tools] to the base sentence . . . hooking devices that preserve us from the tedium of Dick-and-Jane sentences.

—Mina P. Shaughnessy, *Errors and Expectations*

****

You'll never get anywhere with all those darn little short sentences.

—Gregory Clark, *A Social Perspective on the Function of Writing*

Grammar for High School

A Sentence-Composing Approach—
A Student Worktext

DON and JENNY KILLGALLON

HEINEMANN
Portsmouth, NH

Heinemann
361 Hanover Street
Portsmouth, NH 03801–3912
www.heinemann.com

Offices and agents throughout the world

ISBN-10: 0-325-01046-3
ISBN-13: 978-0-325-01046-5

Editor: Lisa Luedeke
Production: Elizabeth Valway
Cover design: Shawn Girsberger
Composition: House of Equations, Inc.
Manufacturing: Jamie Carter

Printed in the United States of America on acid-free paper
17   EBM   13

It's a very ancient saying,
But a true and honest thought,
That if you become a teacher,
By your pupils you'll be taught.

—Richard Rodgers and Oscar Hammerstein,
"Getting to Know You," from *The King and I*

————————

To all our students:
thanks for teaching us what works.

Contents

Activities to learn how to imitate the grammatical tools of great writers. These first steps in sentence imitating will help you learn, practice, and use the fourteen grammatical tools within the rest of this worktext.

A writing toolbox with fourteen sentence-composing tools to build better sentences, resembling those of professional writers.

Practices using two or more of the *same tool* within the same sentence.

Practices using two or more *different tools* within the same sentence.

A focus on the special punctuation practices of authors with activities on learning and applying those practices in your writing.

Contents

Acknowledgments

As you work through this worktext, you will learn grammatical tools used by authors. As a result, you will create your own toolbox for composing sentences, develop your own writing style, and discover your own voice as a writer, while lastingly hearing the whispering of other voices—of Harper Lee, John Steinbeck, Ernest Hemingway, William Golding, and the hundreds of others on the following pages.

We thank all those writers whose model sentences transform literature into a legacy of lessons, providing for you voices of enduring value, voices that will help you discover your own.

Imitating the Grammar of the Greats

Why are the sentences of great authors more interesting, more memorable than the sentences of most people? One big reason is that their sentences are not monotonously alike. A huge difference is the ways those authors build their sentences. The purpose of this worktext is to teach those ways by focusing on the grammatical tools of great authors to build better sentences.

Look at the varied ways these ten sentences are built, all by William Golding, author of the novel *Lord of the Flies*. No two are built the same.

1. He stood knee-deep in the central grass, looking at his hidden feet, trying to pretend that he was in a tent.

2. Half-relieved, half-daunted by the implication of further terrors, the savages murmured again.

3. Percival was mouse-colored and had not been very attractive even to his mother; Johnny was well-built, with fair hair and a natural belligerence.

4. In front of them, only three or four yards away, was a rock-like hump where no rock should be.

5. There was a small pool at the end of the river, dammed back by sand and full of white water-lilies and needle-like reeds.

6. Evening was advancing toward the island; the sounds of the bright fantastic birds, the bee-sounds, even the crying of the gulls that were returning to their roosts among the square rocks, were fainter.

7. He was old enough, twelve years and a few months, to have lost the prominent tummy of childhood, and not yet old enough for adolescence to have made him awkward.

8. Here—and his hands touched grass—was a place to be in for the night, not far from the tribe, so that if the horrors of the supernatural emerged one could at least mix with humans for the time being.

9. The flame, invisible at first in that bright sunlight, enveloped a small twig, grew, was enriched with color, and reached up to a branch, which exploded with a sharp crack.

10. If there was no beast—and almost certainly there was no beast—well and good; but if there was something waiting on top of the mountain, what was the use of three of them, handicapped by the darkness and carrying only sticks?

In the pages of this worktext, you will analyze, study, and then imitate the sentences of many authors whose books are often read by high school students—

including Harper Lee (*To Kill a Mockingbird*), John Steinbeck (*Of Mice and Men*), Ernest Hemingway (*The Old Man and the Sea*), and William Golding (*Lord of the Flies*)—to learn, practice, and use their grammatical tools for building better sentences. With the many practices in *Grammar for High School: A Sentence-Composing Approach*, you create your own personal toolbox of sentence-composing tools to use in writing of all kinds.

And guess what? By the end of the worktext, if you learn the tools covered, you will be able to write ten sentences built just like the ten by William Golding! How? The secret is learning to imitate the grammatical tools of our best writers for building good sentences. In this worktext, you'll learn how.

Okay, let's get started on your way to building better—*much better*—sentences. All you need is your determination to learn to build sentences like those of Harper Lee, John Steinbeck, Ernest Hemingway, and William Golding.

Writers learn to write by paying a certain sort of attention to the works of their great predecessors in the medium of written language, as well as by merely reading them.

—John Barth

Chunking to Imitate

In these exercises you will become aware of meaningful divisions within sentences, an awareness you'll need to imitate model sentences. You will learn that authors compose their sentences one "chunk" or meaningful sentence part at a time.

Directions (Part One): Copy the sentence divided into meaningful chunks.

1a. She made stuffed pork chops / with applesauce and mashed potatoes / and it tasted / like cardboard.

1b. She made stuffed / pork chops with applesauce and mashed / potatoes and it tasted like / cardboard.

Frank McCourt, Teacher Man

2a. The family was grouped by / the front door the / mother's hands resting on her / children's shoulders.

2b. The family was grouped by the front door / the mother's hands resting / on her children's shoulders.

Ian McEwan, Enduring Love

3a. For more than a / century the big business of / Gravesend was lumber, which / was the first big business of New / Hampshire.

3b. For more than a century / the big business of Gravesend / was lumber, / which was / the first big business / of New Hampshire.

John Irving, A Prayer for Owen Meany

Directions (Part Two): Copy the model and then copy the sentence that can be divided into chunks that match the chunks in the model.

1. MODEL: Outside, I found a taxi for her.

Maya Angelou, The Heart of a Woman

    a. Slowly, the cat jumped and landed quietly.
    b. Nearby, Akeelah had a dictionary in hand.

2. MODEL: The man toppled to one side, crumpled against the railing, dead.

   Robert Ludlum, *The Prometheus Deception*

   a. The car, swerving to avoid the child, hit a guardrail, loudly.
   b. The winner jumped from her seat, overwhelmed by the applause, joyous.

3. MODEL: He turned slowly and stood a moment longer, a faceless silhouette against the light.

   Morris West, *The Clowns of God*

   a. Morris spoke quickly and complained a while longer, a disgruntled customer in the manager's office.
   b. Beautifully, Clara sang, winning first place in the contest, her competitors not even close to her talent.

Directions (Part Three): Copy the model and then copy the sentence that imitates it. Then chunk both into the same sentence parts, using slash marks (/).

1. MODEL: It was dark when I got up in the morning, frosty when I followed my breath to school.

   Julia Alvarez, "Snow"

   a. It was early when the bus came by from the school, late when it returned the children to their homes.
   b. It was a fine car, shiny with chrome and paint and sleek in shape, a red convertible designed to have a retro look from the 1950s.

2. MODEL: She wore her coarse, straight hair, which was slightly streaked with gray, in a long braided rope across the top of her head.

   Maya Angelou, *Wouldn't Take Nothing for My Journey Now*

   a. They played the grueling, championship matches, which were completely unpredictable by forecasters, with an amazing energy from the weakest players to the strongest.
   b. The arrangement, beautiful, freshly picked from the garden, smelled of a combination of lilies, sage, and magnolia.

In the following activities, you'll build your sentences like those by authors through imitating their sentence structure but using your own content. To think of what to write, first think of interesting content, maybe a situation or character from a book, movie, TV show, or news event—or use your imagination to create original content.

Directions (Part Four): Match the model and its imitation. Copy both sentences. Then chunk both, using a slash (/) between sentence parts. Finally, write your own imitation of each model.

1. MODEL: The elephant was dying, in great agony, very slowly.

   George Orwell, "Shooting an Elephant"

2. MODEL: In the back room of the laboratory, the white rats in their cages ran and skittered and squeaked.

   John Steinbeck, *Cannery Row*

IMITATIONS

a. Near the old barn by the railroad tracks, the stray cat foraged and lived and slept.

b. The sunset was happening, in silent splendor, quite colorfully.

Unscrambling to Imitate

The unscrambling of sentence parts helps you to see how those parts are connected within the model sentence. As a result, you will glimpse the mind of an author composing a sentence so you can go through a similar process when you compose sentences.

Directions: Unscramble the sentence parts to imitate the model. Then write your own imitation of the model.

1. MODEL: Dumpster diving is outdoor work, often surprisingly pleasant.

   Lars Eighner, "On Dumpster Diving"

   a. sometimes quite costly
   b. is recreational activity
   c. mall strolling

2. MODEL: Near the cab, idling in front of the mortuary, was a huge Oldsmobile.

   Stephen King, *Hearts in Atlantis*

   a. was a skittering gecko
   b. behind the pool
   c. zigzagging in back of the cabana

3. MODEL: Above the fields and pastures, the mountains were just becoming visible as the morning fog burned away.

   Charles Frazier, *Cold Mountain*

   a. were just becoming interested
   b. when the fire alarm sounded
   c. after the cartoons and previews
   d. the kids

4. MODEL: In the shallows, the dark, water-soaked sticks and twigs, smooth and old, were undulating in clusters on the bottom against the clean ribbed sand.

E. B. White, "Once More to the Lake"

    a. sweet and tasty
    b. were beckoning to children
    c. in their kiddie seats within their mom's grocery carts
    d. on that aisle
    e. the tempting, brightly colored candies and lifesavers

Combining to Imitate

These exercises ask you to combine a series of plain sentences into just one varied sentence by changing the plain sentences into sentence parts resembling the model sentence. As you do these exercises, you'll become aware that plain sentences can easily be changed into sentence parts of better, more varied sentences.

Directions: Combine the following sentences to create a sentence that has the same order of sentence parts as the model. Then write your own imitation of the model.

1. MODEL: Twisting and punching and kicking, the two boys rolled across the floor.

    Lois Duncan, *A Gift of Magic*

    a. The winning team was laughing and yelling and celebrating.
    b. The team cavorted.
    c. The cavorting was inside the locker room.

2. MODEL: He fell back, exhausted, his ankle pounding.

    Ralph Ellison, "Flying Home"

    a. She raced fast.
    b. She was determined.
    c. Her lungs were bursting.

3. MODEL: Alone, Tom looked around the room and knew that he was a stranger here.

    Hal Borland, *When the Legends Die*

    a. Clark was afraid.
    b. Clark walked down the alley.
    c. Clark hoped something.
    d. Clark hoped that he was alone there.

4. MODEL: The room was empty, a silent world of sinks, drain boards, and locked cupboards.

Frank Bonham, Chief

    a. The arena was full.
    b. The arena was a huge cavern.
    c. It was filled with fans.
    d. It was filled with bright lights.
    e. And it was filled with exciting music.

Imitating Alone

Once you have learned how to imitate professional sentences, you will be able to imitate almost any professional sentence just by seeing how the model is built and then building your own sentence in a similar way.

Directions: Write an imitation of each model sentence, one sentence part at a time. Read one of your imitations to see if your classmates can guess which model you imitated.

Models:

1. Quietly, / carefully, / she stepped around her / to wake the fire.

   Toni Morrison, *Beloved*

2. To keep ourselves / from going crazy / from boredom, / we tried / to think of word games.

   Barbara Kingsolver, *The Bean Trees*

3. All the American guests / were carrying their plates / into the living room, / while all the Iranian guests / remained standing / around the buffet table.

   Anne Tyler, *Digging to America*

4. Before the store opened, / he sat on a step / of the loading platform, / observing a black beetle / struggling on its back / on the concrete / of the parking lot.

   John Updike, *Terrorist*

Using the Sentence-Composing Toolbox

The sentence-composing toolbox is the heart of this worktext. It teaches fourteen grammatical tools authors use in their sentences that you can use within your own sentences. Although some tools may be new to you, all of them are easy to learn, practice, and use to enhance your writing.

Words	Review These Pages
Opening adjective	14–17

Example: Powerless, we witnessed the sacking of our launch.

> Pierre Boulle, *Planet of the Apes*

Delayed adjective	18–21

Example: People under the helicopter ducked down, **afraid**, as if they were being visited by a plague or a god.

> Barbara Kingsolver, *Animal Dreams*

Opening adverb	22–25

Example: Unfairly, we poked fun at him, often in his presence.

> Sue Miller, *While I Was Gone*

Delayed adverb	26–29

Example: These crazy Saints stared out at the world, **wildly**, like lunatics.

> Alice Walker, *In Search of Our Mothers' Gardens*

Phrases	Review These Pages
Absolute phrase	34–38

Example: Two hard-faced men, **both cradling submachine guns**, stood watching him closely from the adjacent guard station.

> Robert Ludlum, *The Moscow Vector*

Appositive phrase	40–43

Example: A bald, slight man, he reminded me of a baby bird.

> Tracy Chevalier, *The Girl with a Pearl Earring*

Prepositional phrase   44–47

Example: The angry man chased Mikey and me **around the yellow house** and **up a backyard path, under a low tree, up a bank, through a hedge, down some snowy steps,** and **across the grocery store's delivery driveway.**

Annie Dillard, *An American Childhood*

Participial phrase   48–52

Example: Clearing his throat loudly, he stepped out from behind the bookshelves.

J. K. Rowling, *Harry Potter and the Chamber of Secrets*

Gerund phrase   54–57

Example: Making new friends didn't come easily, but in time he developed a skill at that.

Robert Ludlum, *The Prometheus Deception*

Infinitive phrase   58–62

Example: To get his feet wet in such a freezing temperature meant trouble and danger.

Jack London, "To Build a Fire"

Clauses   **Review These Pages**

Clause types (independent, dependent)   68–73

Example: <u>Suddenly, Alfred,</u> **who had heard the fight from across the street,** <u>attacked from the rear with his favorite weapon, an indoor ball bat.</u> *(independent is underlined; dependent is bolded.)*

John Steinbeck, *Cannery Row*

Adjective clause   74–78

Example: Stunned, Jem and I looked at each other, then at Atticus, **whose collar seemed to worry him.**

Harper Lee, *To Kill a Mockingbird*

Adverb clause   80–84

Example: One leg was gone, and the other was held by tendons, and part of the trouser and stump twitched and jerked **as though it were not connected.**

Ernest Hemingway, *A Farewell to Arms*

Noun clause   86–89
Example: The most insidious thing about Ronnie was **that weak minds found him worth imitating.**

Stephen King, *Hearts in Atlantis*

Format for the Tools

Definition—A concise, clear grammatical description of the tool, with tips to identify the tool.

Examples—Professional sentences containing the tool **in bold type**.

Varied Practices—After an introductory matching exercise, the sentence-composing techniques—unscrambling, combining, imitating, expanding—vary the ways in which the tool is practiced.

Section Tool Review—At the end of each section—words, phrases, clauses—you will review the tools by studying how they are used by a famous author: Harper Lee (*words*), John Steinbeck (*phrases*), Ernest Hemingway (*clauses*).

Creative Writing—After each review section, you will apply what you've learned to improve paragraphs by building better sentences. To improve the paragraphs, you'll use your new tools plus others you've previously learned.

Sentence-Composing Tools: Opening Adjective

DEFINITION —————————————————————————————

An adjective at the opening of a sentence. An adjective is any descriptive word that can fit into this blank: *Sam is a _____ student.*

Here are a few possibilities to describe the student: *happy, sad, angry, glad, smart, sneaky, polite, disruptive,* etc. Jot down ten more.

An opening adjective may be a single word or the first word in an adjective phrase. An adjective phrase begins with an adjective and then continues the description. Here are examples: *happy to graduate, sad because her pet died, angry at not getting the job, glad about winning the spelling bee, smart as Einstein, sneaky at times, polite with both elders and children, disruptive because he was beside his best friend,* etc. A comma follows an opening adjective, whether a single word or a phrase.

Sentences can contain single or multiple opening adjectives:

Single opening adjective: **Powerless**, we witnessed the sacking of our launch.

Pierre Boulle, Planet of the Apes

Multiple opening adjectives: **Bloodthirsty** and **brutal**, the giants brought themselves to the point of extinction by warring amongst themselves during the last century.

Armstrong Sperry, Call It Courage

Opening adjective phrases: **Numb of all feeling**, **empty as a shell**, still he clung to life, and the hours droned by.

J. K. Rowling, Harry Potter and the Goblet of Fire

PRACTICE 1: MATCHING ————————————————————

Match the opening adjectives with the sentences. Write out each sentence, inserting and underlining the opening adjectives.

Sentences:	Opening Adjectives:
1. ^, I wanted to run away and be gone from this strange place. Keith Donahue, *The Stolen Child*	a. Alive

2. ^, I felt behind me, my hand pleading for that rifle.

    Theodore Waldeck, "Certain, Sudden Death"

b. Hot and dusty and over-wearied

3. ^, the elephant was worth at least a hundred pounds, but dead, he would only be worth the value of his tusks, five pounds, possibly.

    George Orwell, "Shooting an Elephant"

c. Lonesome

4. ^, he rocked his own body back and forth, breathing deeply to release the remembered pain.

    Lois Lowry, *The Giver*

d. Able to move now

5. ^, he came to our door and eased his heavy pack and asked for refreshment, and Devola brought him a pail of water from our spring.

    Bill and Vera Cleaver, *Where the Lilies Bloom*

e. Frantic, never turning my head— because the water buffalo had started his charge

PRACTICE 2: UNSCRAMBLING TO IMITATE

In the model and the scrambled list, identify the opening adjective. Next, un-scramble and write out the sentence parts to imitate the model. Finally, write your own imitation of the model and identify the opening adjective.

MODEL: Speechless, Bryson scanned the small living room, frantically.

    Robert Ludlum, *The Prometheus Deception*

a. hopefully

b. spotted the soft inviting sofa

c. Kendra

d. uncomfortable

PRACTICE 3: COMBINING TO IMITATE

In the model, identify the opening adjectives. Next, combine the list of sentences to imitate the model. Finally, write your own imitation of the model and identify any opening adjectives.

MODEL: Dark, velvety, the beauty of his mustache was enhanced by his strong clean-shaven chin.

Toni Morrison, Beloved

a. His cautionary steps were slow.

b. His cautionary steps were weary.

c. His cautionary steps were caused by something.

d. The cause was the surrounding overexcited horses.

PRACTICE 4: IMITATING

Identify the opening adjectives in the models and sample imitations. Then write an imitation of each model sentence, one sentence part at a time. Read one of your imitations to see if your classmates can guess which model you imitated.

Models:

1. Wordless, we split up.

Annie Dillard, An American Childhood

   Sample: Wet, the napkin fell apart.

2. Cold, dark, and windowless, it stretched the length of the house.

Jessamyn West, "The Child's Day"

   Sample: Hot, humid, and muggy, the weather exhausted the stamina of the bikers.

3. Afraid that we might hunt for a cheaper apartment for the next two weeks and find nothing better than this one, we took it.

Wallace Stegner, Crossing to Safety

   Sample: Happy that we would escape to a lovely beach for the upcoming one month and have nothing but good times, we left home.

PRACTICE 5: EXPANDING

The opening adjectives are omitted at the caret mark (^) in the following sentences. For each caret, add an opening adjective or adjective phrase, blending your content and style with the rest of the sentence.

1. ^, I began climbing the ladder's rungs, slightly reassured by having Finny right behind me.

   John Knowles, *A Separate Peace*

2. ^ and ^, he wandered about the many tents, only to find that one place was as cold as another.

   Jack London, *The Call of the Wild*

3. ^ and ^, my limited reading helped me to know something of a world beyond the four walls of my study.

   Christy Brown, *My Left Foot*

Sentence-Composing Tools: Delayed Adjective

DEFINITION

An adjective placed after the word described. An adjective is any descriptive word that can fit into this blank: *Sam is a _____ student.*

Here are a few possibilities to describe the student: *happy, sad, angry, glad, smart, sneaky, polite, disruptive,* etc. Jot down ten more.

A delayed adjective may be a single word or the first word in an adjective phrase. An adjective phrase begins with an adjective and then continues the description. Here are examples: *happy to graduate, sad because her pet died, angry at not getting the job, glad about winning the spelling bee, smart as Einstein, sneaky at times, polite with both elders and children, disruptive because he was beside his best friend,* etc.

Commas punctuate a delayed adjective—one comma if it occurs at the end of the sentence, two if earlier in the sentence.

Sentences can contain single or multiple delayed adjectives:

Single delayed adjective: People under the helicopter ducked down, **afraid**, as if they were being visited by a plague or a god.

> Barbara Kingsolver, *Animal Dreams*

Multiple delayed adjectives: Each snowflake was different, Sister Zoe said, like a person, **irreplaceable** and **beautiful**.

> Julia Alvarez, "Snow"

Delayed adjective phrase: A dog came bounding among us with a loud volley of barks, and leapt round us, **wild with glee at finding so many human beings together**.

> George Orwell, "A Hanging"

PRACTICE 1: MATCHING

Match the delayed adjectives with the sentences. Write out each sentence, inserting and underlining the delayed adjectives.

Sentences:

1. Milk, ^, attracted every small flying thing from gnats to grasshoppers.

> Toni Morrison, *Beloved*

Delayed Adjectives:

a. scarcely able to shovel the mashed potatoes into his mouth

2. It seemed dreadful to see the great beast lying there in agony, ^.

> George Orwell, "Shooting an Elephant"

   b. capable of sorting a hamper full of clothes into five subtly differentiated piles

3. The water in this pool has a dark clarity, like smoked glass, ^.

> Edward Abbey, "Aravaipa Canyon"

   c. sticky and sour on her dress

4. Picture poor old Alfy coming home from football practice every evening, bruised and aching, agonizingly tired, ^.

> Paul Roberts, *Understanding English*

   d. transparent but obscure

5. I am an enthusiastic laundress, ^, but a terrible housekeeper.

> Nancy Mairs, *Plaintext*

   e. powerless to move and yet powerless to die

PRACTICE 2: UNSCRAMBLING TO IMITATE

In the model and the scrambled list, identify the delayed adjectives. Next, unscramble and write out the sentence parts to imitate the model. Finally, write your own imitation of the model and identify the delayed adjectives.

MODEL: They ate like men, ravenous and intent.

> Toni Morrison, *Beloved*

a. They sang like angels.

b. The angels were pure.

c. And the angels were sweet.

PRACTICE 3: COMBINING TO IMITATE

In the model, identify the delayed adjective. Next, combine the list of sentences to imitate the model. Finally, write your own imitation of the model and identify any delayed adjectives.

MODEL: He forgot that his Lesser Warders were watching, afraid to interfere.

Stephen King, *The Eyes of the Dragon*

a. She knew something.

b. What she knew is how her sisters were feeling.

c. Her sisters were happy to help.

PRACTICE 4: IMITATING

Identify the delayed adjectives in the models and sample imitations. Then write an imitation of each model sentence, one sentence part at a time. Read one of your imitations to see if your classmates can guess which model you imitated.

Models:

1. Dumpster diving is outdoor work, often surprisingly pleasant.

Lars Eighner, "On Dumpster Diving"

Sample: Doing homework is necessary discipline, sometimes incredibly helpful.

2. The baby's eyes were the shape of watermelon seeds, very black and cut very precisely into her small, solemn face.

Anne Tyler, *Digging to America*

Sample: The unspoken pain was the weight of river rocks, very heavy and embedded most certainly into her aching, dying body.

3. I shivered as he tossed the feathered corpse of the dead chicken, limp as a cloth, into the back of the truck.

Barbara Kingsolver, *Animal Dreams*

Sample: I stared as he threw the battered ball from the garbage can, smelly as a foot, into the field to the pitcher.

PRACTICE 5: EXPANDING ————————————————————————

The delayed adjectives are omitted at the caret mark (^) in the following sentences. For each caret, add a delayed adjective or adjective phrase, blending your content and style with the rest of the sentence.

1. The man toppled to one side, crumpled against the railing, ^.

    Robert Ludlum, *The Prometheus Deception*

2. The spiders lie on their sides, ^ and ^, their legs drying in knots.

    Annie Dillard, "Death of a Moth"

3. He was twenty-six, dark-haired and ^, ^, ^, and ^.

    John Steinbeck, *Cannery Row*

Sentence-Composing Tools: Opening Adverb

DEFINITION

An adverb at the beginning of a sentence. A comma follows an opening adverb. All adverbs give information about an action.

Adverbs that tell *how* an action happened (*quickly, slowly, rapidly*) always end in *ly*. Other adverbs tell *when* an action happened (*now, then, yesterday*), or *where* an action happened (*overhead, nearby, underneath*).

How: **Unfairly**, we poked fun at him, often in his presence.

> Sue Miller, *While I Was Gone*

When: **Then**, Harry felt as though an invisible pillow had quite suddenly been pressed over his mouth and nose.

> J. K. Rowling, *Harry Potter and the Goblet of Fire*

Where: **Outside**, I found a taxi for her.

> Maya Angelou, *The Heart of a Woman*

Sentences can contain single or multiple opening adverbs:

Single opening adverb: **Incredibly**, the man was still chasing after us.

> Annie Dillard, *An American Childhood*

Multiple opening adverbs: **Then, slowly**, he fell to his knees and pitched forward onto the road, blood pooling red on the black asphalt.

> Robert Ludlum, *The Moscow Vector*

PRACTICE 1: MATCHING

Match the opening adverbs with the sentences. Write out each sentence, inserting and underlining the opening adverbs.

Sentences:

1. ^, to sneak up on a giraffe was far more difficult than I had imagined.

   > Michael Crichton, *Travels*

Opening Adverbs:

a. Curiously

2. ^, he would reach Peter's rooms, let himself quietly in, and go about the early chores, building a fire, making half a dozen breakfast muffins, heating water for tea.

    Stephen King, *The Eyes of the Dragon*

b. Weakly, tentatively

3. ^, the ship rose out of the water, gleaming in the moonlight.

    J. K. Rowling, *Harry Potter and the Goblet of Fire*

c. Slowly, magnificently

4. ^, the dying woman let herself back against the pillows.

    Wallace Stegner, *Crossing to Safety*

d. Promptly at six o'clock

5. ^, in summer and winter, maggots are uncommon in dumpsters.

    Lars Eighner, "On Dumpster Diving"

e. Clearly

PRACTICE 2: UNSCRAMBLING TO IMITATE

In the model and the scrambled list, identify the opening adverb. Next, unscramble and write out the sentence parts to imitate the model. Finally, write your own imitation of the model and identify the opening adverb.

MODEL: Suddenly, Alfred, who had heard the fight from across the street, attacked from the rear with his favorite weapon, an indoor ball bat.

    John Steinbeck, *Cannery Row*

a. sat up in the bed with her nightly snack

b. who had read the novel for over two hours

c. Jasmine

d. afterward

e a mini Oreo cookie

PRACTICE 3: COMBINING TO IMITATE

In the model, identify the opening adverb. Next, combine the list of sentences to imitate the model. Finally, write your own imitation of the model and identify any opening adverbs.

MODEL: Outside, the doctor's car was surrounded by boys while Finny was being lifted inside it by Phil Latham.

John Knowles, *A Separate Peace*

a. This happened inside.

b. The younger children were involved with games.

c. While they were involved, Laura was being tutored near them.

d. The tutoring was by their teacher.

PRACTICE 4: IMITATING

Identify the opening adverbs in the models and sample imitations. Then write an imitation of each model sentence, one sentence part at a time. Read one of your imitations to see if your classmates can guess which model you imitated.

Models:

1. Here, relatives swarmed like termites.

Wallace Stegner, *Crossing to Safety*

Sample: Now, questions buzzed like mosquitoes.

2. Slowly, methodically, miserably, she ate the jellied bread.

Toni Morrison, *Beloved*

Sample: Automatically, repeatedly, steadily, he hammered the final nails.

3. Very slowly and very carefully, Harry got to his feet and set off again as fast as he could without making too much noise, hurrying through the darkness back toward Hogwarts.

J. K. Rowling, *Harry Potter and the Goblet of Fire*

Sample: Very obviously and very intentionally, Maria reached for the candy and ate it as quickly as she could without pausing between pieces, reveling in the mint inside the chocolate.

PRACTICE 5: EXPANDING

The opening adverbs are omitted at the caret mark (^) in the following sentences. For each caret, add an opening adverb, blending your content and style with the rest of the sentence.

1. ^, she came back to the kitchen, carrying Daphne in a white knit romper that showed off her curly black hair.

   Anne Tyler, *Saint Maybe*

2. ^, ^, we began to cut for the autopsy.

   Michael Crichton, *Travels*

3. ^ and ^, they drove through the darkness, and though the rain stopped, the wind rushed by and whistled and made strange sounds.

   Frances Hodgson Burnett, *The Secret Garden*

Sentence-Composing Tools: Delayed Adverb

DEFINITION

An adverb placed after the action described. All adverbs give information about an action.

Adverbs that tell *how* an action happened (*quickly, slowly, rapidly*) always end in *ly*. Other adverbs tell *when* an action happened (*now, then, yesterday*), or *where* an action happened (*overhead, nearby, underneath*).

How: These crazy Saints stared out at the world, **wildly**, like lunatics.
Alice Walker, In Search of Our Mothers' Gardens

When: I wondered how I could have missed noticing, **before**, all those bones.
Barbara Kingsolver, Animal Dreams

Where: By now the sharks were all around us, **above** and **below**, and to all sides.
Michael Crichton, Travels

Sentences can contain single or multiple delayed adverbs:

Single delayed adverb: They smiled, **delicately**, like weary children remembering a party.
John Steinbeck, Cannery Row

Multiple delayed adverbs: He worked himself to death, **finally** and **precisely**, at 3:00 a.m. Sunday morning.
Ellen Goodman, Close to Home

PRACTICE 1: MATCHING

Match the delayed adverbs with the sentences. Write out each sentence, inserting and underlining the delayed adverbs.

Sentences:

1. He stretched out his hands, ^, waving them in the air to ward off the attack from the dinosaur he knew was coming.
   Michael Crichton, Jurassic Park

Delayed Adverbs:

a. noiselessly and smoothly

2. We all had a drink together, native and European alike, quite ^.

    George Orwell, "A Hanging"

    b. noisily

3. In hunting season, all kinds of small game turn up in dumpsters, some of it, ^, not entirely dead.

    Lars Eighner, "On Dumpster Diving"

    c. blindly, frantically

4. She watched the children troop in, ^, an ancient nursery rhyme running through her head.

    Mary Elizabeth Vroman, "See How They Run"

    d. amicably

5. His body glided quietly across the room, ^.

    John Steinbeck, *The Pearl*

    e. sadly

PRACTICE 2: UNSCRAMBLING TO IMITATE

In the model and the scrambled list, identify the delayed adverb. Next, unscramble and write out the sentence parts to imitate the model. Finally, write your own imitation of the model and identify the delayed adverb.

MODEL: As I watched him, he seemed to adjust himself a little, visibly.

    F. Scott Fitzgerald, *The Great Gatsby*

a. a bit

b. she tried to excuse herself

c. when she told him

d. lamely

PRACTICE 3: COMBINING TO IMITATE

In the model, identify the delayed adverbs. Next, combine the list of sentences to imitate the model. Finally, write your own imitation of the model and identify any delayed adverbs.

MODEL: The cars traveled Reynolds Street, slowly and evenly.

Annie Dillard, An American Childhood

a. The girl crossed a street.

b. The street was Washington Avenue.

c. She crossed the street confidently.

d. And she crossed the street purposefully.

PRACTICE 4: IMITATING

Identify the delayed adverbs in the models and sample imitations. Then write an imitation of each model sentence, one sentence part at a time. Read one of your imitations to see if your classmates can guess which model you imitated.

Models:

1. Still winded, Smith sat up, slowly.

Robert Ludlum, The Moscow Vector

Sample: Almost finished, Peter speeded up, triumphantly.

2. We explored the streams, quietly, where the turtles slid off the sunny logs and dug their way into the soft lake bottom.

E. B. White, "Once More to the Lake"

Sample: We walked the streets, dreamily, where the sun set in the crystal sky and melted its way over the inky black skyscrapers.

3. He was clambering, heavily, among the creepers and broken trunks, when a bird, a vision of red and yellow, flashed upwards with a witch-like cry.

William Golding, Lord of the Flies

Sample: She was running, desperately, between the road and railroad tracks, after a car, her hope for escape and rescue, passed by with an oblivious driver.

PRACTICE 5: EXPANDING

The delayed adverbs are omitted at the caret mark (^) in the following sentences. For each caret, add a delayed adverb, blending your content and style with the rest of the sentence.

1. The elephant was dying, in great agony, very ^.

   George Orwell, "Shooting an Elephant"

2. We touched the sheets covering the corpse, ^, at the edge of the fabric.

   Michael Crichton, *Travels*

3. Griffin was light and fast, his gloves a red blur tapping away at Alfred's face, ^ and ^ as rain on a roof.

   Robert Lipsyte, *The Contender*

REVIEWING THE TOOLS: HARPER LEE'S *TO KILL A MOCKINGBIRD*

Directions: Using these abbreviations, identify the underlined tools. If you need to review the tool, study the pages listed.

Words	Review These Pages
opening adjective = OADJ	14–17
delayed adjective = DADJ	18–21
opening adverb = OADV	23–25
delayed adverb = DADV	26–29

REVIEW 1: IDENTIFYING

Directions: Write the abbreviation of the underlined tool. Each sentence illustrates either an opening adjective (OADJ) or an opening adverb (OADV).

1. <u>Dimly</u>, I saw Atticus pushing papers from the table into his briefcase.

2. <u>Comfortable</u>, I lay on my back and waited for sleep, and while waiting I thought of Dill.

3. <u>Suddenly to my left</u>, I noticed that the men were backing away from Miss Maudie's house, moving down the street toward us.

4. <u>Slowly, painfully</u>, the ten dollars was collected.

5. <u>Upright and uncompromising</u>, Aunt Alexandra was sitting in a rocking chair exactly as if she had sat there every day of her life.

Directions: Write the abbreviation of the underlined tool. Each sentence illustrates either a delayed adjective (DADJ) or a delayed adverb (DADV).

6. When Atticus switched on the overhead light in the living room, he found Jem at the window, <u>pale except for the vivid mark of the screen on his nose</u>.

7. Tim Johnson, the mad dog, came into sight, <u>dazedly</u>, walking in the inner rim of the curve parallel to the Radley house.

8. The back porch was bathed in moonlight, and the shadow, <u>crisp as toast</u>, moved across the porch toward Jem.

9. Jem opened the gate, <u>slowly as possible</u>, lifting it aside and resting it on the fence.

10. Jem was standing outside in the cold beside Atticus, <u>groggy and tousled</u>, holding his overcoat closed at the neck, his other hand jammed into his pocket.

REVIEW 2: IMITATING

The following model sentences contain the four tools you just reviewed—*opening adjective, opening adverb, delayed adjective, delayed adverb*—as well as other kinds of sentence-composing tools. For each model sentence, write the letter of its imitation. Then write your own imitation of the same model.

Model Sentences:

1. The old Radley house was the same, droopy and sick, but as we stared down the street, we thought we saw an inside shutter move.

2. Safely on our porch, panting and out of breath, we looked back.

3. Sunburned, lanky, they seemed to be all farmers, but this was natural because townfolk rarely sat on juries.

4. Atticus kept us in fits that evening, enjoyably, reading columns of print about a man who sat on a flagpole for no discernible reason.

5. His hair was dead and thin, almost feathery on top of his head.

Imitations:

A. Overgrown, wild, they looked like weeds, but this was only because the flowers never appeared in March.

B. Taylor slept in a tent that night, nervously, hearing the sounds of wolves in the night who howled from the darkness in the distance.

C. Megan's voice was high and squeaky, nearly birdlike in the back of her throat.

D. The dilapidated old barn was still there, musty and morose, but as Jeremy approached near the building, he thought he heard a secret inhabitant whimper.

E. Belatedly in her remarks, stuttering and just in time, she thanked them.

REVIEW 3: CREATING

In Harper Lee's *To Kill a Mockingbird*, three children—Jem, his little sister Scout, and their friend Dill—are fascinated by the legend of Boo Radley.

Inside the Radley house lived a malevolent phantom [Boo Radley]. People said he went out at night when the moon was down, and peeped in windows. When people's azaleas froze in a cold snap, it was because he had breathed on them. Boo was about six-and-a-half feet tall, judging from his tracks; he dined on raw squirrels and any cats he could catch. That's why his hands were bloodstained—if you ate an animal raw, you could never wash the blood off. There was a long jagged scar that ran across his face; what teeth he had were yellow and rotten; his eyes popped, and he drooled most of the time.

"The Shadow" is based on an incident in *To Kill a Mockingbird*: one night, Jem, Scout, and Dill sneak up on the house of the mysterious Boo Radley to look in a window, hoping to catch a glimpse of him.

At the caret (^), use your imagination to add opening adjectives, opening adverbs, delayed adjectives, or delayed adverbs to make the paragraph good enough to appear in the original novel!

"The Shadow"

(1) ^, Jem, Scout, and Dill spit on the hinge of the gate into the Radley property so it wouldn't squeak, ^. (2) ^, Jem inched toward the Radley house, and climbed the stairs of the back porch, ^. (3) ^, Scout and Dill watched, ^. (4) ^, a moving shadow appeared on the wall of the porch behind Jem, approaching, ^, closer and closer to him. (5) With slow movement like a terrible phantom, the shadow produced horror and pounding hearts in Scout and Dill, who knew that Jem was unaware of its presence, ^. (6) ^, before the shadowy figure reached him, Jem, ^, bolted down the porch steps, and ran fast as lightning, ^, scrambling toward the safety of his house, but, ^, climbing clumsily under the Radley's barbed wire fence, he got his pants caught and became stuck.

Sentence-Composing Tools: Absolute Phrase

DEFINITION

A sentence part describing the rest of the sentence in which it appears. Absolutes are *almost* complete sentences. As a test, you can make *every* absolute a sentence by adding *was* or *were*.

Examples:

1. A teenager in a black tank top, **a greenish tattoo flowing across her broad back**, hoisted a toddler onto her shoulder.

   Barbara Kingsolver, Animal Dreams

   Test: A greenish tattoo *was* flowing across her broad back.

2. Two hard-faced men, **both cradling submachine guns**, stood watching him closely from the adjacent guard station.

   Robert Ludlum, The Moscow Vector

   Test: Both *were* cradling submachine guns.

Another way to identify an absolute is by its opening word, which is often a possessive pronoun: *my, his, her, its, our, their.* The pronoun can be stated (visible) or implied (invisible).

Visible possessive pronoun: Mama was out of bed now, **her long black skirt [WAS] over her nightgown.** *(The pronoun* her *is visible before* long black skirt.*)*

John Steinbeck, "Flight"

Invisible possessive pronoun: He was sitting on his cot, **elbows [WERE] on knees**, looking down. *(The word* his *is invisible before* elbows.*)*

John Knowles, A Separate Peace

Sentences can contain single or multiple absolute phrases:

Single absolute: He looked over to where the huge, filthy birds sat, **their naked heads sunk in the hunched feathers.**

Ernest Hemingway, "The Snows of Kilimanjaro"

Multiple absolutes: She burst into great sobs, **her whole body shaking, tears streaming down her face**.

Michael Crichton, *Travels*

Note: Absolute phrases can be removed without destroying the basic meaning of the sentence, but notice how including them adds detail and style to the sentences. Absolutes build better sentences.

1a. A teenager in a black tank top hoisted a toddler onto her shoulder.

1b. A teenager in a black tank top, **a greenish tattoo flowing across her broad back**, hoisted a toddler onto her shoulder.

2a. Two hard-faced men stood watching him closely from the adjacent guard station.

2b. Two hard-faced men, **both cradling submachine guns**, stood watching him closely from the adjacent guard station.

3a. He looked over to where the huge, filthy birds sat.

3b. He looked over to where the huge, filthy birds sat, **their naked heads sunk in the hunched feathers**.

PRACTICE 1: MATCHING

Match the absolute phrases with the sentences. Write out each sentence, inserting and underlining the absolute phrases.

Sentences:

1. He clapped twice, like a schoolteacher calling the children to attention, and she was up and stumbling, ^.

    Ann Patchett, *Bel Canto*

2. The little boy stared at her silently, ^.

    Flannery O'Connor, "The River"

3. He foresaw that mankind might split into two species, ^.

    Kenneth Brower, *The Starship and the Canoe*

4. The poor little row of forget-me-nots along the wall came out bravely, ^.

    Christy Brown, *My Left Foot*

5. The dinosaur ran, ^, leaving prints six inches deep wherever it settled its weight.

    Ray Bradbury, "A Sound of Thunder"

Absolute Phrases:

a. his nose and eyes running

b. its pelvic bones crushing aside trees and bushes, its taloned feet clawing damp earth

c. one following the technological path which he described, the other holding on as best it could to the ancient folkways of natural living

d. their tiny starlike blossoms all blue and white and speckled red

e. her left foot asleep

PRACTICE 2: UNSCRAMBLING TO IMITATE

In the model and the scrambled list, identify the absolute phrase. Next, unscramble and write out the sentence parts to imitate the model. Finally, write your own imitation of the model and identify the absolute phrase.

MODEL: The motorcycle on the sidewalk speeded up and skidded obliquely into a plate-glass window, the front wheel bucking and climbing the brick base beneath the window.

Frank Rooney, "Cyclist's Raid"

a. and ending the dance on the final beat

b. stepped quickly

c. the couple spinning

d. the last pair in the dance contest

e. and swirled rhythmically to the Latin song

PRACTICE 3: COMBINING TO IMITATE

In the model, identify the absolute phrase. Next, combine the list of sentences to imitate the model. Finally, write your own imitation of the model and identify the absolute phrase.

MODEL: Gerard, his elbows spread wide on the arms of his chair, stretched his legs further under the table and looked at the fire.

Elizabeth Bowen, "Foothold"

a. This sentence is about Liam.

b. He had his pants hiked up above the surface of the water.

c. He moved his feet further into the lake.

d. And he waded toward his dog.

PRACTICE 4: IMITATING

Identify the absolute phrases in the models and sample imitations. Then write an imitation of each model sentence, one sentence part at a time. Read one of your imitations to see if your classmates can guess which model you imitated.

Models:

1. The dragon came crashing and blundering out of the underbrush, its scales glowing a greenish copper color, its soot-caked nostrils venting smoke.

Stephen King, *The Eyes of the Dragon*

   Sample: The toddler went bobbing and weaving across the room, her voice gurgling a sweet rhythmic coo, her candy-covered fingers feeling sticky.

2. I saw the mouse vanish in the general direction of my apartment house, his little body quivering with fear in the great open sun on the blazing concrete.

Loren Eiseley, "The Brown Wasps"

Sample: I heard Mrs. Saffire yell at the noisy little kid in the neighbor's yard, her shrill scream rising in decibels in the calm, quiet stillness of the early morning.

3. Striding along the sidewalk under the Martian sun, tall, smiling, eyes amazingly clear and blue, came a young man of some twenty-six years.

> Ray Bradbury, *The Martian Chronicles*

Sample: Standing inside the doorway under the glaring light, vulnerable, cowering, body incredibly rigid and fearful, was a small rabbit from some lost warren.

PRACTICE 5: EXPANDING

The absolute phrases are omitted at the caret mark (^) in the following sentences. For each caret, add an absolute phrase, blending your content and style with the rest of the sentence.

1. The dead man's face was coated with mud, ^, ^.

> George Orwell, "Shooting an Elephant"

2. Ted Munday perched like a giant grasshopper on the balcony, ^, ^.

> John Le Carre, *Absolute Friends*

3. ^, ^, I made it to the hotel desk.

> Wallace Stegner, *Crossing to Safety*

Sentence-Composing Tools: Appositive Phrase

DEFINITION

A noun phrase identifying a person, place, or thing named in a sentence. Appositives often begin with the words *a*, *an*, or *the*. They always answer one of these questions:

Who is he? Who is she? Who are they? *(people)*

What is it? What are they? *(places or things)*

Examples:

Identifying people: Harry was small and tough, **a boy going through life with his chin stuck out a mile.**

Stephen King, Hearts in Atlantis

Identifying places: I walked along Gilman Street, **the best street in town.**

John Knowles, A Separate Peace

Identifying things: The furniture, **a mixture of Logan crafted walnut and oak,** included a walnut bed whose ornate headboard rose halfway up the wall toward the high ceiling.

Mildred D. Taylor, Roll of Thunder, Hear My Cry

Sentences can contain single or multiple appositive phrases:

Single appositive: **A bald slight man,** he reminded me of a baby bird.

Tracy Chevalier, The Girl with a Pearl Earring

Multiple appositives: Most of the town's natives did their shopping on King Street, **the town's shopping strip, a slice of chain department stores, auto dealerships, fast-food restaurants.**

Tracy Kidder, Home Town

Note: Appositive phrases can be removed without destroying the basic meaning of the sentence, but notice how including them adds detail and style to the sentences. Appositives build better sentences.

1a. Harry was small and tough.

1b. Harry was small and tough, **a boy going through life with his chin stuck out a mile**.

2a. I walked along Gilman Street.

2b. I walked along Gilman Street, **the best street in town**.

3a. The furniture included a walnut bed whose ornate headboard rose halfway up the wall toward the high ceiling.

3b. The furniture, **a mixture of Logan crafted walnut and oak**, included a walnut bed whose ornate headboard rose halfway up the wall toward the high ceiling.

PRACTICE 1: MATCHING

Match the appositive phrases with the sentences. Write out each sentence, inserting and underlining the appositive phrases.

Sentences:

1. There was no one in The Hot Spot store but Mr. Shiftlet and the boy behind the counter, ^.

   Flannery O'Connor, "The Life You Save May Be Your Own"

2. Once they were in her office, ^, Professor McGonagall motioned to Harry and Hermione to sit down.

   J. K. Rowling, *Harry Potter and the Prisoner of Azkaban*

3. In our clenched fists, we held our working cards from the shop, ^.

   Gerda Weissmann Klein, "All But My Life"

4. Gen Watanabe, ^, leaned over and spoke the words in Japanese to his employer.

   Ann Patchett, *Bel Canto*

5. A gray cat, dragging its belly, crept across the lawn, and a black one, ^, trailed after.

   Katherine Mansfield, "Bliss"

Appositive Phrases:

a. a small room with a large, welcoming fire

b. the young man who worked as Mr. Hosokawa's translator

c. its shadow

d. those sacred cards that we thought meant security

e. a pale youth with a greasy rag hung over his shoulder

PRACTICE 2: UNSCRAMBLING TO IMITATE

In the model and the scrambled list, identify the appositive phrase. Next, unscramble and write out the sentence parts to imitate the model. Finally, write your own imitation of the model and identify the appositive phrase.

MODEL: The proprietor, a little gray man with an unkempt mustache and watery eyes, leaned on the counter, reading a newspaper.

John Steinbeck, *The Grapes of Wrath*

a. a tall thin blonde

b. walked down the runway

c. with a long mane and long legs

d. the model

e. eyeing the audience

PRACTICE 3: COMBINING TO IMITATE

In the model, identify the appositive phrase. Next, combine the list of sentences to imitate the model. Finally, write your own imitation of the model and identify the appositive phrase.

MODEL: A veteran bronc rider, Tom Black has ridden nine horses to death in the rodeo arena, and at every performance the spectators expect him to kill another one.

Hal Borland, *When the Legends Die*

a. This sentence is about a fascinating historical speaker, Professor Southwick.

b. He has visited many museums.

c. He visits them for study of the medieval period.

d. And at every visit the curators want him to give another lecture.

PRACTICE 4: IMITATING

Identify the appositive phrases in the models and sample imitations. Then write an imitation of each model sentence, one sentence part at a time. Read one of your imitations to see if your classmates can guess which model you imitated.

Models:

1. A golden female moth, a biggish one with a two-inch wingspread, flapped in

the fire of the candle, drooped abdomen into the wet wax, stuck, flamed, and frazzled in a second.

Annie Dillard, "Death of a Moth"

Sample: A green garter snake, a skittish one with a six-inch length, slid toward the foot of the tree, parted grass in the wet yard, stopped, sensed, and disappeared in a flash.

2. The dictionary had a picture of an aardvark, a long-tailed, long-eared, burrowing African mammal living off termites caught by sticking out its tongue as an anteater does for ants.

Malcolm X and Alex Haley, *The Autobiography of Malcolm X*

Sample: The living room contained a portrait of an ancestor, a grim-faced, black-haired dour matronly relative giving out disapproval signaled by looking down her nose as a parent does in disappointment.

3. A beautiful animal, it lay in the position of a marble lion, its head toward a man sitting on an upturned bucket outside the cage.

Frank Bonham, *Chief*

Sample: A shy observer, she hesitated on the outskirts of the spirited group, her body behind a flirty girl talking with a handsome boy inside the circle.

PRACTICE 5: EXPANDING

The appositive phrases are omitted at the caret mark (^) in the following sentences. For each caret, add an appositive phrase, blending your content and style with the rest of the sentence.

1. Vivi had a summer earache, ^.

Rebecca Wells, *Ya Yas in Bloom*

2. A few days after I went into the hospital for that crick in my neck, another brother, ^, was undergoing spinal surgery in the same hospital two floors above me.

John McMurtry, "Kill 'Em! Crush 'Em! Eat 'Em Raw!"

3. ^, William T. Stead seemed almost to have planned his arrival on deck later that night when the Titanic hit the iceberg.

Walter Lord, *A Night to Remember*

43

Sentence-Composing Tools: Prepositional Phrase

DEFINITION ————————————————————————————————

A preposition is the first word in a prepositional phrase. Here are common prepositions: *about, above, across, after, along, at, before, behind, below, beyond, by, down, except, from, in, inside, like, near, off, on, over, outside, to, through, under, up, upon, with, within, without.*

Any word that will fit in this blank is a preposition: **It was _____ the box;** *about the box, at the box, beyond the box, from the box, near the box, over the box, under the box, inside the box, outside the box, by the box,* etc.

Prepositional phrases can be *single, connected (a series of two or more in a row),* or **multiple** *(two or more in the same position but—unlike connected phrases—separated by commas):*

Examples:

Single prepositional phrase: **In the beginning,** God created the heaven and the earth.

The Bible

Connected prepositional phrases: The whole congregation prayed for me alone, **in a mighty wail of moans and voices.** *(a series of two connected prepositional phrases:* in a mighty wail *and* of moans and voices*)*

Langston Hughes, The Big Sea

Multiple prepositional phrases: The angry man chased Mikey and me **around the yellow house and up a backyard path, under a low tree, up a bank, through a hedge, down some snowy steps,** and **across the grocery store's delivery driveway.** *(seven prepositional phrases in a row, separated by commas)*

Annie Dillard, An American Childhood

Note: Prepositional phrases can be removed without destroying the basic meaning of the sentence, but notice how including them adds detail and style to the sentences. Prepositional phrases build better sentences.

1a. God created the heaven and the earth.

1b. **In the beginning,** God created the heaven and the earth.

2a. The whole congregation prayed for me alone.

2b. The whole congregation prayed for me alone, **in a mighty wail of moans and voices.**

3a. The angry man chased Mikey and me.

3b. The angry man chased Mikey and me **around the yellow house** and **up a backyard path, under a low tree, up a bank, through a hedge, down some snowy steps,** and **across the grocery store's delivery driveway.**

PRACTICE 1: MATCHING

Match the prepositional phrases with the sentences. Write out each sentence, inserting and underlining the prepositional phrases. Tell the kind of prepositional phrase: single, connected, or multiple.

Sentences:

1. ^, the mountains were just becoming visible as the morning fog burned away.

   Charles Frazier, *Cold Mountain*

2. ^ came an old Chinaman.

   John Steinbeck, *Cannery Row*

3. Our first year in New York we rented a small apartment with a Catholic school nearby, taught by the Sisters of Charity, hefty women in long black gowns and bonnets that made them look peculiar, ^.

   Julia Alvarez, "Snow"

4. By 5:00 p.m. of the afternoon of the funeral, the company president had begun, discreetly of course, ^, to make inquiries about his replacement.

   Ellen Goodman, *Close to Home*

5. ^, there was no way to move products of any size from the territories in the West to markets on the East Coast or in Europe.

   Stephen E. Ambrose, *Nothing Like It in the World*

Prepositional Phrases:

a. without railroads or rivers

b. like dolls in mourning

c. above the fields and pastures

d. down the hill, past the Palace Flophouse, down the chicken walk, and through the vacant lot

e. with care and taste

PRACTICE 2: UNSCRAMBLING TO IMITATE

In the model and the scrambled list, identify the prepositional phrases. Next, unscramble and write out the sentence parts to imitate the model. Finally, write your own imitation of the model and identify the prepositional phrases.

MODEL: In the daytime, in the hot mornings, these outboard motor boats made a petulant, irritable sound.

E. B. White, "Once More to the Lake"

a. during the flower festival

b. wore their insincere, frozen smiles

c. those dainty gloved matrons

d. on the veranda

PRACTICE 3: COMBINING TO IMITATE

In the model, identify the prepositional phrases. Next, combine the list of sentences to imitate the model. Finally, write your own imitation of the model and identify the prepositional phrases.

MODEL: Both FDR and Truman were men of exceptional determination, with great reserves of personal courage and cheerfulness.

David McCullough, *Truman*

a. This sentence is about both laughter and tears.

b. Both laughter and tears are signs of deep emotion.

c. Those signs are with contrasting feelings.

d. Those emotions are of intense happiness or sadness.

PRACTICE 4: IMITATING

Identify the prepositional phrases in the models and sample imitations. Then write an imitation of each model sentence, one sentence part at a time. Read one of your imitations to see if your classmates can guess which model you imitated.

Models:

1. Throughout dinner Lucille has been careening wildly from sadness to elation to despair.

   Audrey Niffenegger, *The Time Traveler's Wife*

   Sample: On New Year's eve the crowd had been celebrating constantly from nine o'clock to midnight to dawn.

2. Franny was looking at a little warm blotch of sunshine, about the size of a poker chip, on the tablecloth.

   J. D. Salinger, *Franny and Zooey*

   Sample: Bernard was listening to a bright cheerful sonata of Beethoven, about the length of a TV show, on the stereo.

3. About a year after the incident, Tommy was talking to a former gang member named Felix, a young man he'd known as a baby.

   Tracy Kidder, *Home Town*

   Sample: In the aisle near the computers, Kelly was looking at a super cell phone on sale, a versatile model he'd seen in an ad.

PRACTICE 5: EXPANDING

The prepositional phrases are omitted at the caret mark (^) in the following sentences. For each caret, add a prepositional phrase, blending your content and style with the rest of the sentence.

1. ^, old roses were dying.

   Toni Morrison, *Beloved*

2. I despised team sports, spending some of the wretchedest afternoons of my life sweaty and humiliated, ^ and ^.

   Nancy Mairs, *Plaintext*

3. Woodbridge College, ^, was a small school, but it exuded a sense of quiet prosperity, ^.

   Robert Ludlum, *The Prometheus Deception*

Sentence-Composing Tools: Participial Phrase

DEFINITION

A verbal ending in *ing* or *ed* used to describe. A verbal is a verb that also works like another part of speech. Participles show action, so they act like verbs, but they also describe, so they act like adjectives.

Present participles always end in *ing*. Unlike *ing* main verbs, which cannot be removed from a sentence, participles are removable.

Verb (not removable): He was **clearing his throat loudly**.

Present participle (verbal, removable): **Clearing his throat loudly**, he stepped out from behind the bookshelves.

J. K. Rowling, *Harry Potter and the Chamber of Secrets*

Difference Between Present Participles and Gerunds: Like present participles, gerunds (pages 54–57) are verbals that also end in *ing*, but it's easy to tell the difference. Present participles are removable sentence parts; gerunds are not. In each pair, the first contains a present participle, and the second contains a gerund. Notice that only the present participles can be removed.

1a. *Feeling so much better after the nap*, Gunster dressed and went out.

1b. *Feeling so much better after the nap* relieved Gunster.

2a. Ralston, *going down the staircase backward*, was very unsteady.

2b. The cause of Ralston's fall was *going down the staircase backward*.

3a. The damaged plane landed poorly, *skidding left and right with sparks flying everywhere*.

3b. The captain during touchdown worried about *skidding left and right with sparks flying everywhere*.

Past participles usually end in *ed*. Unlike *ed* main verbs, which cannot be removed from a sentence, past participles are removable. *Note:* Most past participles end in *ed*; others—by far the minority—end in *en* (*forgiven*) or end irregularly (*sung*). This worktext treats only the most common—those with *ed*—because once you learn the *ed* participles, you will understand and use the others.

Verb (not removable): A wide pink ribbon was **tied in back with a bow.**

Past participle (verbal, removable): Around her waist was a wide pink ribbon, **tied in back with a bow.**

Bill Brittain, The Wish Giver

Authors sometimes use multiple participial phrases within the same sentence:

Present participles: The men within the door stared at one another, **shifting on their boots, twiddling their fingers,** and **holding onto their hip belts.** *(three)*

Ray Bradbury, The Martian Chronicles

Past participles: **Hated by the Federalists** and **suspected by the Republicans,** John Quincy Adams returned to private life. *(two)*

John F. Kennedy, Profiles in Courage

Both present and past participles: **Curled up inside a big one-meter drainage pipe that ran under the road,** she had her baseball glove in her mouth, and she was rocking back and forth, **banging her head repeatedly against the back of the pipe.** *(one past participle and one present participle)*

Michael Crichton, Jurassic Park

Participial phrases can be removed without destroying the basic meaning of the sentence, but notice how including them adds detail and style to the sentences. Participles build better sentences.

1a. He stepped out from behind the bookshelves.

1b. **Clearing his throat loudly,** he stepped out from behind the bookshelves.

2a. Around her waist was a wide pink ribbon.

2b. Around her waist was a wide pink ribbon, **tied in back with a bow.**

3a. She had her baseball glove in her mouth, and she was rocking back and forth.

3b. **Curled up inside a big one-meter drainage pipe that ran under the road,** she had her baseball glove in her mouth, and she was rocking back and forth, **banging her head repeatedly against the back of the pipe.**

Using the Sentence-Composing Toolbox

PRACTICE 1: MATCHING

Match the participial phrases with the sentences. Write out each sentence, inserting and underlining the participial phrases.

Sentences:

1. Many birds and crocodiles swallowed small stones, which collected in a muscular pouch in the digestive tract, ^.

    Michael Crichton, *Jurassic Park*

2. She was trying to teach me to smile, ^.

    J. D. Salinger, *Raise High the Roof Beam, Carpenters*

3. Grampa, ^, had succeeded in buttoning the buttons of his blue shirt into the button-holes of his underwear.

    John Steinbeck, *The Grapes of Wrath*

4. ^, Harry blinked and looked down at the floor.

    J. K. Rowling, *Harry Potter and the Goblet of Fire*

5. His tutor, ^, listened to George's violin with a radio earplug in place.

    Kenneth Brower, *The Starship and the Canoe*

Participial Phrases:

a. addicted to baseball

b. blinded by the blaze of the spells that had blasted from every direction, deafened by a series of bangs

c. called the gizzard

d. spreading the muscles around my mouth with her fingers

e. fumbling with his chest

PRACTICE 2: UNSCRAMBLING TO IMITATE

In the model and the scrambled list, identify the participial phrases. Next, unscramble and write out the sentence parts to imitate the model. Finally, write your own imitation of the model and identify the participial phrases.

MODEL: The elephant was tearing up bunches of grass, beating them against his knees to clean them and stuffing them into his mouth.

George Orwell, "Shooting an Elephant"

a. on pieces of garbage

b. chopping them with their teeth to soften them

c. the mice were dining

d. and sniffing them for fresh scents

PRACTICE 3: COMBINING TO IMITATE

In the model, identify the participial phrases. Next, combine the list of sentences to imitate the model. Finally, write your own imitation of the model and identify the participial phrases.

MODEL: Not daring to glance at the books, I went out of the library, fearing that the librarian would call me back for further questioning.

Richard Wright, Black Boy

a. I was not thinking to hide in the box.

b. I stood behind the door.

c. I was knowing that my sister would discover me there.

d. She would discover me after little searching.

PRACTICE 4: IMITATING

Identify the participial phrases in the models and sample imitations. Then write an imitation of each model sentence, one sentence part at a time. Read one of your imitations to see if your classmates can guess which model you imitated.

Models:

1. Blinded and confused, the mouse was running straight away from his field.

Loren Eiseley, "The Brown Wasps"

Sample: Dejected and disheartened, the girl was backing slowly away from this challenge.

2. The sun was coming over the ridge now, glaring on the whitewash of the houses and barns, making the wet grass blaze softly.

John Steinbeck, The Red Pony

Sample: The child was peeking around the door silently, looking at the smiles on the teachers and parents, hearing their gentle laughter sound quietly.

3. We caught two bass, hauling them in briskly as though they were mackerel, pulling them over the side of the boat in a business-like manner without any landing net, and stunning them with a blow on the back of the head.

E. B. White, "Once More to the Lake"

Sample: I chose the tabby kitten, picking it up gently as though it were breakable, putting it into the pocket of my coat in a gentle motion without any jerky movement, and holding it like a secret in the core of my heart.

PRACTICE 5: EXPANDING

The participial phrases are omitted at the caret mark (^) in the following sentences. For each caret, add a participial phrase, blending your content and style with the rest of the sentence.

1. My teachers wished me to write accurately, ^ and ^.

Kurt Vonnegut, "How to Write with Style"

2. Children love to play in piles of leaves, ^, ^.

Diane Ackerman, *A Natural History of the Senses*

3. Hours of wintertime had found me in the treehouse, ^, ^, ^, ^, ^.

Harper Lee, *To Kill a Mockingbird*

Sentence-Composing Tools: Gerund Phrase

DEFINITION

A verbal ending in *ing* used to name activities. A verbal is a verb that also works like another part of speech. Gerunds show action, so they act like verbs, but they also name, so they act like nouns by naming activities.

To see how gerunds act like nouns, insert any of these phrases into any of the blanks: *playing chess, learning new things, climbing mountains in distant lands, building sand castles on the beach, taking a computer apart to investigate its guts*, etc.

1. _____ is fun. *(subject)*

2. We like _____. *(direct object)*

3. They talked about _____. *(object of preposition)*

4. A great leisure activity is _____. *(predicate noun)*

5. Their favorite pastime, _____, is enjoyed by many. *(appositive)*

Difference Between Gerunds and Present Participles: Like gerunds, present participles (pages 48–52) are verbals that end in *ing*, but it's easy to tell the difference. Present participles can be removed from the sentence without destroying the sentence, but gerunds cannot be removed without destroying the sentence. In each pair, the first contains a present participle, and the second contains a gerund. Notice that only the present participles can be removed.

1a. *Feeling so much better after the nap*, Gunster dressed and went out.

1b. *Feeling so much better after the nap* relieved Gunster.

2a. Ricky, *going down the staircase backward*, was very unsteady.

2b. His mom had warned Ricky about *going down the staircase backward*.

3a. The damaged plane landed poorly, *skidding left and right with sparks flying everywhere*.

3b. The captain during touchdown worried about *skidding left and right with sparks flying everywhere*.

Sentences can contain single or multiple gerund phrases:

Single gerund: **Making new friends** didn't come easily, but in time he developed a skill at that.

Robert Ludlum, The Prometheus Deception

Multiple gerunds: My mother told me about **dressing in her best party clothes on Saturday nights** and **going to the town's plaza to promenade with her girlfriends in front of the boys they liked.**

Ortiz Cofer, "The Myth of the Latin Woman"

PRACTICE 1: MATCHING

Match the gerund phrases with the sentences. Write out each sentence, inserting and underlining the gerund phrases.

Sentences:

1. Building the railroad involved ^.
   Stephen E. Ambrose, *Nothing Like It in the World*

2. God had not struck Westley dead for ^.
   Langston Hughes, *The Big Sea*

3. ^ is literally an expression of your differences, or agreements of opinion, with the author.
   Mortimer Adler, "How to Mark a Book"

4. In the process of ^ we must not be guilty of wrongful deeds.
   Martin Luther King Jr., "I Have a Dream"

5. Getting old is just a matter of ^.
   Barbara Kingsolver, *Pigs in Heaven*

Gerund Phrases:

a. making notes in the margins of a book

b. getting easier to see through until all your failing insides are in plain view and everyone's business

c. building a grade, laying ties, laying rails, spiking in rails, filling in ballast

d. gaining our rightful place

e. taking His name in vain or for lying in the temple

PRACTICE 2: UNSCRAMBLING TO IMITATE

In the model and the scrambled list, identify the gerunds. Next, unscramble and write out the sentence parts to imitate the model. Finally, write your own imitation of the model and identify the gerunds.

MODEL: We had to pray without ceasing and work without tiring.

Maya Angelou, *The Heart of a Woman*

a. and

b. to study without tiring

c. we had

d. listen without daydreaming

PRACTICE 3: COMBINING TO IMITATE

In the model, identify the gerund phrase. Next, combine the list of sentences to imitate the model. Finally, write your own imitation of the model and identify the gerund phrase.

MODEL: After making ten paper birds, Sadako lined them up on the table beside the golden crane.

Eleanor Coerr, *Sadako and the Thousand Paper Cranes*

a. This happened before taking the nasty medicine.

b. Before he took it, James put it down.

c. He put it on the sink.

d. He put it down near the toothpaste tube.

PRACTICE 4: IMITATING

Identify the gerund phrases in the models and sample imitations. Then write an imitation of each model sentence, one sentence part at a time. Read one of your imitations to see if your classmates can guess which model you imitated.

Models:

1. After untangling himself, he ran to the wall.

Mark Bowden, *Black Hawk Down*

Sample: For preparing herself, she listened to the music.

2. He remembered seeing the blood bursting through that man's fingers in a flood, drenching his uniform.

Stephen King, *Hearts in Atlantis*

Sample: He anticipated hearing the applause filling up the entire theater in a wave, fulfilling his dream.

3. Feeding our bellies seemed a more vital job to us than trying to feed our minds.

    Christy Brown, *My Left Foot*

Sample: Sharing my mind was a more acceptable activity to me than attempting to share my heart.

PRACTICE 5: EXPANDING

The gerund phrases are omitted at the caret mark (^) in the following sentences. For each caret, add a gerund phrase, blending your content and style with the rest of the sentence.

1. Some parents, upon ^, had their hair turn white overnight, were stunned into catatonia, heart attacks, or sudden death.

    Keith Donohue, *The Stolen Child*

2. I remember the bitter fifth-grade conflict I touched off by ^ and ^.

    Jon Katz, "How Boys Become Men"

3. ^ and ^ were routine procedures, and Eliza lost her horror of blood and learned to stitch human flesh as calmly as formerly she had embroidered sheets for her trousseau.

    Isabel Allende, *Daughter of Fortune*

Sentence-Composing Tools: Infinitive Phrase

DEFINITION

A verbal that always begins with *to* plus a verb: *to sing, to read, to linger, to laugh, to sigh, to study,* etc. A verbal is a verb that also works like another part of speech—a noun, an adjective, or an adverb.

Infinitives can name something (like nouns), describe something (like adjectives), or give a reason for something (like adverbs). Infinitives convey action, so they act like verbs, but also at the same time they act like nouns, adjectives, or adverbs.

Examples:

1. *Noun infinitive:* **To make it to the final round of the playoffs** was the team's goal. *(The infinitive names the team's goal.)*

2. *Adjective infinitive:* The coach emphasized the need **to make it to the final round of the playoffs**. *(The infinitive describes the need.)*

3. *Adverb infinitive:* The team from Western High School worked overtime **to make it to the final round of the playoffs**. *(The infinitive gives the reason the team worked overtime.)*

Sentences can contain single or multiple infinitives:

Single Infinitives:

1. **To get his feet wet in such a freezing temperature** meant trouble and danger. *(noun infinitive—names what meant trouble and danger)*

   Jack London, "To Build a Fire"

2. Suddenly, she had an almost overwhelming desire **to see what was behind the other doors and down the other corridors**. *(adjective infinitive—describes the desire)*

   Hal Borland, *When the Legends Die*

3. Back through the vegetable garden he went, and he paused for a moment **to smash a green muskmelon with his heel**, but he was not happy about it. *(adverb infinitive—states the reason he paused)*

   John Steinbeck, *The Red Pony*

Multiple Infinitives:

4. At nine o'clock Earth started **to explode, to catch fire**, and **to burn**. *(noun infinitives—name what started)*

> Ray Bradbury, *The Martian Chronicles*

5. It was the time **to accomplish his mission** or **to fail**. *(adjective infinitives—describe the time)*

> Walter Dean Myers, *Legend of Tarik*

6. She lingered a moment or two **to bathe her own face with the cool water** and **to smooth her hair**. *(adverb infinitives—state the reason she lingered)*

> Gaston Leroux, *The Phantom of the Opera*

Many infinitive phrases can be removed without destroying the basic meaning of the sentence, but notice how including them adds detail and style to the sentences. Infinitives build better sentences.

1a. Suddenly, she had an almost overwhelming desire.

1b. Suddenly, she had an almost overwhelming desire **to see what was behind the other doors and down the other corridors**.

2a. Back through the vegetable garden he went, and he paused for a moment, but he was not happy about it.

2b. Back through the vegetable garden he went, and he paused for a moment **to smash a green muskmelon with his heel**, but he was not happy about it.

3a. She lingered a moment or two.

3b. She lingered a moment or two **to bathe her own face with the cool water** and **to smooth her hair**.

PRACTICE 1: MATCHING

Match the infinitive phrases with the sentences. Write out each sentence, inserting and underlining the infinitive phrases.

Sentences:

1. My mother told me about dressing in her best party clothes on Saturday nights and going to the town's plaza ^.

   Ortiz Cofer, "The Myth of the Latin Woman"

2. Seventeenth century European women and men sometimes wore beauty patches in the shape of hearts, suns, moons, and stars, applying them to their breasts and faces, ^.

   Diane Ackerman, "The Face of Beauty"

3. ^, they went in single file, with Frodo leading.

   J. R. R. Tolkien, *The Lord of the Rings: The Fellowship of the Ring*

4. When Ulysses S. Grant and Robert E. Lee met in the parlor of a modest house at Appomattox Court House, Virginia, on April 9, 1865, ^, a great chapter in American life came to a close, and a great new chapter began.

   Bruce Catton, "Grant and Lee: A Study in Contrasts"

5. The trick of growing up is ^.

   Keith Donohue, *The Stolen Child*

Infinitive Phrases:

a. to prevent their getting separated and wandering in different directions

b. to remember to grow

c. to work out the terms for the surrender of Lee's Army of Northern Virginia

d. to promenade with her girlfriends in front of the boys they liked

e. to draw an admirer's eye away from any imperfections, which, in that era, too often included smallpox scars

PRACTICE 2: UNSCRAMBLING TO IMITATE

In the model and the scrambled list, identify the infinitive phrases. Next, unscramble and write out the sentence parts to imitate the model. Finally, write your own imitation of the model and identify the infinitive phrases.

MODEL: I wanted to explain that I'd hunted for him in the evening and to apologize for not having known him in the garden.

F. Scott Fitzgerald, *The Great Gatsby*

a. to lie that she'd waited for the letter for a month

b. for not having opened it during her vacation

c. and to rationalize

d. Fredericka began

PRACTICE 3: COMBINING TO IMITATE

In the model, identify the infinitive phrases. Next, combine the list of sentences to imitate the model. Finally, write your own imitation of the model and identify the infinitive phrase.

MODEL: To avoid embarrassment and to make the job easier, all students quickly learned certain interviewing tricks.

Michael Crichton, *Travels*

a. The first purpose was to garner respect.

b. And the second purpose was to make his employees happier.

c. To achieve those two purposes, the boss periodically distributed compliments.

d. The compliments were appropriate, and they were earned.

PRACTICE 4: IMITATING

Identify the infinitive phrases in the models and sample imitations. Then write an imitation of each model sentence, one sentence part at a time. Read one of your imitations to see if your classmates can guess which model you imitated.

Models:

1. To lose one's name is the beginning of forgetting.

   Keith Donohue, *The Stolen Child*

   Sample: To dance a samba is the epitome of rhythm.

2. A child is a guest in the house, to be loved and respected, never possessed, since he or she belongs to God.

   J. D. Salinger, *Raise High the Roof Beam, Carpenters*

   Sample: A dessert is the finale of the meal, to be savored and appreciated, never rushed, because it lingers in memory.

3. We need to involve more citizens in the fight against drugs, to increase pressure on drug criminals, and to build on anti-drug programs that have proved to work.

   William Bennett, "Should Drugs Be Legalized?"

   Sample: We need to encourage our children in the process of living, to acknowledge growth in moral development, and to reward those productive behaviors that have led to success.

PRACTICE 5: EXPANDING

The infinitive phrases are omitted at the caret mark (^) in the following sentences. For each caret, add an infinitive phrase, blending your content and style with the rest of the sentence.

1. To ^, a writer has to develop a special kind of reading skill.

   Donald M. Murray, "The Maker's Eye: Revising Your Own Manuscripts"

2. It was a place to ^, a place to ^.

   John Steinbeck, *Cannery Row*

3. The only way to keep playing professional football was to ^, to ^, to ^, and to ^.

   John McMurtry, "Kill 'Em! Crush 'Em! Eat 'Em Raw!"

REVIEWING THE TOOLS: JOHN STEINBECK'S *OF MICE AND MEN* ─────────

Directions: Using these abbreviations, identify the underlined tools. If you need to review the tool, study the pages listed.

Phrases	Review These Pages
absolute phrase= AB	34–38
appositive phrase= AP	40–43
prepositional phrase = PREP	44–47
participial phrase (present or past) = P	48–52
gerund phrase = G	54–57
infinitive phrase = INF	58–62

REVIEW 1: IDENTIFYING ──────────────────────────

Directions: Write the abbreviation of the underlined tool.

1. George, <u>sitting on the bunk beside Lennie</u>, frowned as he thought.
2. <u>In the stable buck's room</u>, a small electric globe threw a meager yellow light.
3. A water snake slipped along on the pool, <u>its head held up like a little periscope</u>.
4. Curley's wife lay on her back, <u>covered with hay</u>.
5. For a moment, Crooks did not see him, but on <u>raising his eyes</u> he stiffened, and a scowl came on his face.
6. George stacked the scattered cards and began <u>to lay out his solitaire hand</u>.
7. At that moment a young man came into the bunk house, <u>a thin young man with a brown face, brown eyes, and a head of tightly curled hair</u>.

Directions: Write the abbreviation of each underlined tool. Each sentence illustrates a combination of tools from the six tools listed here.

Example:

Sentence: There is a path (A) <u>through the willows</u> and (B) <u>among the sycamores</u>, (C) <u>a path beaten hard by boys coming down from the ranches</u> (D) <u>to swim in the deep pool</u>.

Answers:

(A)—PREP (prepositional)   (C)—AP

(B)—PREP (prepositional)   (D)—INF

8. (A) <u>Near one wall</u> there was a black cast-iron stove, (B) <u>its stovepipe going straight up through the ceiling</u>.

9. In the middle of the room stood a big square table, (A) <u>littered with playing cards</u>, and around it were grouped boxes for the players (B) <u>to sit on</u>.

10. Slowly, (A) <u>like a terrier</u> who doesn't want (B) <u>to bring a ball to its master</u>, Lennie approached, drew back, approached again.

11. He subsided, (A) <u>grumbling to himself</u>, (B) <u>threatening the future cats which might dare</u> (C) <u>to disturb the future rabbits</u>.

12. Behind him walked his opposite, (A) <u>a huge man</u>, shapeless of face, (B) <u>with large, pale eyes</u>, (C) <u>with wide sloping shoulders</u>.

13. She stood still (A) <u>in the doorway</u>, (B) <u>smiling a little at them</u>, (C) <u>rubbing the nails of one hand with the thumb and forefinger of the other</u>.

14. Slim was a jerkline skinner, (A) <u>the prince of the ranch</u>, capable of (B) <u>driving ten, sixteen, even twenty mules with a single line</u> (C) <u>to the leaders</u>.

15. The sound of the approaching grain teams was louder, (A) <u>the thud of big hooves on hard ground</u>, (B) <u>the drag of brakes</u>, and (C) <u>the jingle of trace chains</u>.

REVIEW 2: IMITATING

The model sentences contain the six tools you just reviewed—absolute, appositive, prepositional, participial, gerund, infinitive—as well as other kinds of sentence-composing tools. For each model sentence, write the letter of its imitation. Then write your own imitation of the same model.

Model Sentences:

1. Noiselessly, Lennie appeared in the open doorway and stood there looking in, his big shoulders nearly filling the opening.

2. He unrolled his bindle and put things on the shelf, his razor and a bar of soap, his comb and bottle of pills, his liniment and leather wristband.

3. The dog struggled lamely to the side of the room and lay down, grunting softly to himself and licking his grizzled, moth-eaten coat.

4. Old Candy, the swamper, came in and went to his bunk, and behind him struggled his old dog.

5. These shelves were loaded with little articles, soap and talcum powder, razors, and those Western magazines ranch men love to read and scoff at and secretly believe.

Imitations:

A. Little Mattie, the youngest, toddled over and sat on the sofa, and beside her sat her older sister.

B. Her cabinet was filled with various cosmetics, lipstick and eyeliner, mascara, and those false eyelashes teenage girls like to buy and experiment with and sometimes wear.

C. She got out her bag and gathered items for the weekend, her bathing suit and a bottle of suntan lotion, her shorts, a case with makeup, her shirt and team sweatshirt.

D. Gleefully, Maya ran through the sprinkler, and ran back lingering inside, her tiny feet always running in place.

E. The diver walked carefully to the end of the board and balanced there, talking inwardly to himself and rehearsing his intricate championship dive.

REVIEW 3: CREATING

John Steinbeck's *Of Mice and Men* tells the story of two homeless ranch-hands. George, of average size and normal intelligence, is the caretaker of Lennie, of huge size and low intelligence.

> They walked in single file down the path. George was small and quick, dark of face, with restless eyes and sharp, strong features. Every part of him was defined: small, strong hands, slender arms, a thin and bony nose. Behind George walked Lennie, his opposite, a huge man shapeless of face, with large, pale eyes, with wide sloping shoulders who walked heavily, dragging his feet a little, the way a bear drags his paws. George stopped short in the clearing, and Lennie nearly ran over him.

"The Gentle Pulverizer" on page 66 is based upon this incident in *Of Mice and Men*:

> Lennie, a strong man with a childlike mind and heart but the body of a giant, reluctantly fights Curley, a mean little guy who picks fights. Curley starts cruelly hitting the innocent Lennie, but Lennie, fearful that George will disapprove, doesn't fight back. However, when Curley draws blood from Lennie, and keeps pounding him with his fists, George finally yells to Lennie, "Get 'em, Lennie!" Lennie then grabs Curley's fist in midair and clenches it until it's almost pulverized.

At the caret (^), use your imagination to add these phrases—absolute, appositive, prepositional, participial, gerund, infinitive—to make the paragraph good enough to appear in the original novel!

"The Gentle Pulverizer"

(1) At George's signal, Lennie grabbed in his huge hand Curley's fist in midpunch, ^, and held on with a steel grip. (2) ^, the giant Lennie squeezed the fist until Curley was shaking uncontrollably as the pain in his shattered hand exploded. (3) ^, Lennie held on but looked with childlike terror for approval at his caretaker, George, ^. (4) George, ^, yelled for Lennie to release Curley, but at first Lennie held tight, ^. (5) One of Lennie's eyes had been badly cut, ^, and his face was bloodied. (6) Curley, whose broken hand was trapped in Lennie's powerful grip, began to cry from his almost pulverized fist, ^, and Lennie, ^, suddenly let go of him, ^.

Sentence-Composing Tools: Clause Types

DEFINITION

Clauses are groups of words containing subjects and verbs. An independent clause can stand alone as a complete sentence. A dependent clause cannot stand alone because it is only a *part* of a sentence, not a complete sentence. Dependent clauses must link to independent clauses for their full meaning.

All sentences have at least one independent clause—frequently more—and many sentences also have dependent clauses.

There are three kinds of dependent clauses, taught later in this worktext: adjective clause (pages 74–78), adverb clause (pages 80–84), and noun clause (pages 86–89).

Removability Test for Dependent Clauses: All three dependent clauses add detail and style to sentences, but to tell the difference among them, use the "removability test." Adjective clauses and adverb clauses are removable from the sentence in which they appear, but noun clauses are nonremovable. *Important:* this is just a test to tell the difference among the three dependent clauses. Your goal is to add a variety of dependent clauses to your sentences to achieve a more professional style.

In the following sentences, independent clauses are <u>underlined</u>, and dependent clauses are in **boldface**.

1. **When you speak and write**, <u>there is no law that says you have to use big words</u>. *(The dependent clause—an adverb clause—is removable.)*
   Richard Lederer, *The Miracle of Language*

2. <u>Suddenly, Alfred</u>, **who had heard the fight from across the street**, <u>attacked from the rear with his favorite weapon, an indoor ball bat</u>. *(The dependent clause—an adjective clause—is removable.)*
   John Steinbeck, *Cannery Row*

3. **Whatever she planted** <u>grew as if by magic</u>. *(The dependent clause—a noun clause—is nonremovable.)*
   Alice Walker, *In Search of Our Mothers' Gardens*

4. <u>He saw **that I was looking at him**</u>, so <u>he closed his eyes, sleepily, angelically, then stuck out his tongue</u>. *(The dependent clause—a noun clause—is nonremovable.)*
   J. D. Salinger, "For Esme—with Love and Squalor"

5. I will tell you **what Gandalf heard, although Bilbo did not understand it**. *(The first dependent clause—a noun clause—is nonremovable. The second dependent clause—an adverb clause—is removable.)*

J. R. R. Tolkien, The Hobbit

Examples: Sentences with Only Independent Clauses

1. <u>Two nine-year-old boys, neighbors and friends, were walking home from school</u>. *(Contains one independent clause.)*

Jon Katz, "How Boys Become Men"

2. <u>Working desperately, technicians were able to gradually reduce the size of the gas bubble using a special apparatus brought in from the atomic laboratory at Oak Ridge, Tennessee</u>, and <u>the danger of a catastrophic release of radioactive materials subsided</u>. *(Contains two independent clauses joined by* and.*)*

Barry Commoner, The Politics of Energy

3. <u>A little corn was raised on the sterile slope</u>, and <u>it grew short and thick under the wind</u>, and <u>all the cobs formed on the landward sides of the stalks</u>. *(Contains three independent clauses joined by* and.*)*

John Steinbeck, "Flight"

Examples: Sentences with Independent Clauses and Dependent Clauses

4. <u>Catherine had loaded her oilcloth satchel with the leftovers from Sunday dinner</u>, and <u>we were enjoying a breakfast of cake and chicken</u> **when gunfire slapped through the woods**. *(adverb clause)*

Truman Capote, The Grass Harp

5. <u>No one spoke at supper</u>, and <u>his mother</u>, **who sat next to him**, <u>leaned her head in her hand all through the meal, curving her fingers over her eyes so as not to see him</u>. *(adjective clause)*

Gina Berriault, "The Stone Boy"

6. <u>I thought of</u> **how quickly dry timber becomes a roaring fire from a single spark**. *(noun clause)*

Eugenia Collier, "Sweet Potato Pie"

7. **When the children went on a hike**, <u>she packed bird and flower guides into their knapsacks and quizzed them on their return to see</u> **if they had learned anything**. *(adverb clause, noun clause)*

Wallace Stegner, *Crossing to Safety*

Many dependent clauses can be removed without destroying the basic meaning of the sentence, but notice how including them adds detail and style to the sentences. Dependent clauses build better sentences.

1a. Catherine had loaded her oilcloth satchel with the leftovers from Sunday dinner, and we were enjoying a breakfast of cake and chicken.

1b. Catherine had loaded her oilcloth satchel with the leftovers from Sunday dinner, and we were enjoying a breakfast of cake and chicken **when gunfire slapped through the woods**.

2a. Suddenly, Alfred attacked from the rear with his favorite weapon, an indoor ball bat.

2b. Suddenly, Alfred, **who had heard the fight from across the street**, attacked from the rear with his favorite weapon, an indoor ball bat.

3a. There is no law that says you have to use big words.

3b. **When you speak and write**, there is no law that says you have to use big words.

PRACTICE 1: MATCHING

Match the dependent clauses with the sentences. Write out each sentence, inserting and underlining the dependent clauses.

Sentences:

1. ^, your readers will surely feel that you care nothing about them.

   Kurt Vonnegut, "How to Write with Style"

2. By passing through the heart, the electric current during the death penalty distorts normal ventricular rhythm into an ineffective wormlike wriggling called fibrillation, ^.

   Sherman B. Nuland, "Cruel and Unusual"

Dependent Clauses:

a. unless the insect happens to touch one of its legs

b. that you have read actively

3. Tarantulas apparently have little or
no sense of hearing, for a hungry
tarantula will pay no attention to a
loudly chirping cricket placed in
its cage ^.

   Alexander Petrunkevitch, "The Spider and the Wasp"

c. which has the same effect as cardiac
arrest

4. Five score years ago, a great American,
in ^, signed the "Emancipation
Proclamation."

   Martin Luther King Jr., "I Have a Dream"

d. if you scribble your thoughts any
which way

5. If, when you've finished reading a
book, the pages are filled with your
notes, you know ^.

   Mortimer Adler, "How to Mark a Book"

e. whose symbolic shadow we stand

PRACTICE 2: UNSCRAMBLING TO IMITATE

In the model and the scrambled list, identify the independent and dependent
clauses. Next, unscramble and write out the sentence parts to imitate the model.
Finally, write your own imitation of the model and identify independent and dependent clauses.

MODEL: Over lunch, Beattie talked about her older sister, who had lived with her
since her retirement and who was addicted to the shopping network.

   Sue Miller, *While I Was Gone*

a. and which was loved by the high school students

b. which had grown with the addition of twenty stores

c. Jeremy cruised by the shopping mall

d. after school

PRACTICE 3: COMBINING TO IMITATE

In the model, identify the independent and dependent clauses. Next, combine the
list of sentences to imitate the model. Finally, write your own imitation of the
model and identify the independent and dependent clauses.

MODEL: That I had come this far undetected as a changeling for their real son caused me no small satisfaction, but I was not completely at ease.

Keith Donohue, *The Stolen Child*

a. This sentence is about how I had climbed the mountain.

b. I had climbed it uninjured as a novice in this dangerous sport.

c. How I had climbed it made me feel a false confidence.

d. And I was too sure of myself.

PRACTICE 4: IMITATING

Identify the independent and dependent clauses in the models and sample imitations. Then write an imitation of each model sentence, one sentence part at a time. Read one of your imitations to see if your classmates can guess which model you imitated.

Models:

1. I knew that I looked and felt and probably smelled like a cigar butt in a spittoon.

Wallace Stegner, *Crossing to Safety*

Sample: She regretted that he counted and organized and eternally straightened like a tidy cook in a kitchen.

2. Before she fell into a deep, dreamless sleep, she just lay quiet, smiling at the ceiling.

J. D. Salinger, *Franny and Zooey*

Sample: After he dove into the clear, cold water, he just felt great, gliding like a dolphin.

3. He shared a room for years with his older brother Jack, who was big, handsome, and wild.

Tracy Kidder, *Home Town*

Sample: She invented a story for others about her now dead father, who was wealthy, powerful, and adoring.

PRACTICE 5: EXPANDING

The clauses are omitted at the caret mark (^) in the following sentences. For each caret, add the indicated kind of clause (independent or dependent), blending your content and style with the rest of the sentence.

1. ^, which proudly advertised hot and cold running water. *(Add an independent clause.)*

    Michael Crichton, *Travels*

2. In the afternoon, when ^, Mary sometimes gave tea parties for the neighborhood cats. *(Add a dependent clause.)*

    John Steinbeck, *Cannery Row*

3. As ^, a large amount of yellowish-green liquid burst forth, which ^. *(Add two dependent clauses.)*

    J. K. Rowling, *Harry Potter and the Goblet of Fire*

Sentence-Composing Tools: Adjective Clause

DEFINITION ─────────────────────────────────

A dependent clause that describes a person, place, or thing. (For more about dependent clauses, see pages 68–73.) Like all clauses, adjective clauses contain a subject and its verb.

Adjective clauses are descriptive attachments to independent clauses and are, therefore, dependent clauses. They often begin with one of these words: *who, which, whose* called *relative pronouns*.

Who: I sleep with two cats, **who sleep on my legs.**

Annie Dillard, "Death of a Moth"

Which: The good news is that we Americans are governed under a unique Constitution, **which allows us to write whatever we please without fear of punishment.**

Kurt Vonnegut, "How to Write with Style"

Whose: Stunned, Jem and I looked at each other, then at Atticus, **whose collar seemed to worry him.**

Harper Lee, *To Kill a Mockingbird*

Nonrestrictive vs. Restrictive Adjective Clauses:

Nonrestrictive (<u>describes</u> a person, place, or thing, and is punctuated with commas): We run bare-legged to the beach, **which lies smooth, flat, and glistening with fresh wet shells after the night's tides.**

Anne Morrow Lindbergh, *Gift from the Sea*

The nonrestrictive adjective clause doesn't identify the beach; it describes it. Nonrestrictive clauses need commas. Because there is a pause before "which lies smooth, flat, and glistening with fresh wet shells after the night's tides," a comma is needed.

Restrictive (<u>identifies</u> a person, place, or thing and is not punctuated with commas): Already we knew that there was one room in that region above stairs **which no one had seen in forty years.**

William Faulkner, "A Rose for Emily"

The restrictive adjective clause identifies the specific room. What room? The room is restricted to the one "which no one had seen in forty years." Restrictive clauses do not need commas.

In this worktext, only nonrestrictive adjective clauses with commas are practiced because they are the kind that add descriptive detail to your writing.

Sentences can contain single or multiple adjective clauses:

Single Adjective Clause:

1. He misses his sisters and cousins, **who have known him since he was a strong, good-looking boy.**

   Barbara Kingsolver, *Pigs in Heaven*

2. Sully, **whose skills were already maturing**, moved up from the Wolves level to the Lions.

   Stephen King, *Hearts in Atlantis*

3. They gave me a cable knit sweater and an oilskin jacket, **which kept me dry on the wettest days.**

   Keith Donohue, *The Stolen Child*

Multiple Adjective Clauses:

4. To Richardson, **whose nerves were tingling and twitching like live wires,** and **whose heart jolted inside him**, this pause was a long horror.

   Stephen Crane, "Horses—One Dash"

5. She failed to see a shadow, **which followed her like her own shadow, which stopped when she stopped,** and **which started again when she did.**

   Gaston Leroux, *The Phantom of the Opera*

6. These are the men of chemistry, **who spray the trees against pests, who sulfur the grapes, who cut out diseases and rots, mildews, and sicknesses.**

   John Steinbeck, *The Grapes of Wrath*

Adjective clauses can be removed without destroying the sentence, but notice how including them adds detail and style to the sentences. Adjective clauses build better sentences.

1a. I sleep with two cats.

1b. I sleep with two cats, **who sleep on my legs.**

2a. The good news is that we Americans are governed under a unique Constitution.

2b. The good news is that we Americans are governed under a unique Constitution, **which allows us to write whatever we please without fear of punishment.**

3a. Stunned, Jem and I looked at each other, then at Atticus.

3b. Stunned, Jem and I looked at each other, then at Atticus, **whose collar seemed to worry him.**

PRACTICE 1: MATCHING

Match the adjective clauses with the sentences. Write out each sentence, inserting and underlining the adjective clauses.

Sentences:

1. His black hair, ^, was dry now and blowing.

    J. D. Salinger, "The Laughing Man"

2. Ragno ate only flies, ^.

    Keith Donohue, *The Stolen Child*

3. Grabbing the weapon from the limp fingers, he sprung to his feet and began firing wildly in the general direction of the running man, ^.

    Robert Ludlum, *The Prometheus Deception*

4. Sometimes one finds in fossil stones the imprint of a leaf, long since disintegrated, ^.

    Diane Ackerman, *A Natural History of the Senses*

5. Out of the hole came an old battle-torn bull gopher, ^.

    John Steinbeck, *Cannery Row*

Adjective Clauses:

a. who stopped to fire back

b. which had been combed wet earlier in the day

c. who mauled and bit the little gopher so badly that he crept home to his burrow and lay in his great chamber for three days recovering

d. whose outlines remind us how detailed, vibrant, and alive are the things of this earth that perish

e. which he plucked from spider webs

PRACTICE 2: UNSCRAMBLING TO IMITATE

In the model and the scrambled list, identify the adjective clause. Next, unscramble and write out the sentence parts to imitate the model. Finally, write your own imitation of the model and identify the adjective clause.

MODEL: Everyone except Jon, whose nickname was Chuck, talked incessantly.

> Maya Angelou, *The Heart of a Woman*

a. whose job was leader

b. no one but Shanique

c. argued

d. convincingly

PRACTICE 3: COMBINING TO IMITATE

In the model, identify the adjective clause. Next, combine the list of sentences to imitate the model. Finally, write your own imitation of the model and identify the adjective clause.

MODEL: On the fishing trip, I took my son, who had never had any fresh water up his nose and who had seen lily pads only from train windows.

> E. B. White, "Once More to the Lake"

a. Into the field, I led my friend.

b. It was the friend who had never felt any falling crystals on her face.

c. And it was the friend who had known fresh snow only from emailed pictures.

PRACTICE 4: IMITATING

Identify the adjective clauses in the models and sample imitations. Then write an imitation of each model sentence, one sentence part at a time. Read one of your imitations to see if your classmates can guess which model you imitated.

Models:

1. One figure, whose wounds were so dreadful that he more resembled meat than man, tried to rise but could not.

> Charles Frazier, *Cold Mountain*

Sample: One child, whose smile was so bright that she seemed more angelic than human, started to enter and look around.

2. Sally, who would have liked working and who watched our budget with a miser's eye, put a card on the departmental bulletin board advertising that she typed theses and term papers.

   Wallace Stegner, *Crossing to Safety*

Sample: Kim, who would have said nothing and who covered our tracks with a practiced skill, stopped an intruder in the dark foyer claiming that he cleaned apartments and small offices.

3. I saw that my old friend, who had outfoxed Dearie and Ebersole and the Dean of Men, who had gone around and begged his teachers to help him, who had taught me to drink beer by the pitcher and curse in a dozen different intonations, was crying a little bit.

   Stephen King, *Hearts in Atlantis*

Sample: I heard that the new kid, who had threatened Blackie and Sanjay and other members of Cobra, who had made promises and asked other students to join him, who had shown us to stand up for ourselves and respond with a confident, loud voice, was getting a big audience.

PRACTICE 5: EXPANDING

The adjective clauses are omitted at the caret mark (^) in the following sentences. For each caret, add an adjective clause, blending your content and style with the rest of the sentence.

1. He was quite tanned, and his hair, which ^, was a little sun-bleached on top.

   J. D. Salinger, "The Laughing Man"

2. The orchards, whose ^, suddenly bloomed, all at once.

   Barbara Kingsolver, *Animal Dreams*

3. John, who ^, falls in love with Mary, and Mary, who ^, feels sorry for him because he's worried about his hair falling out.

   Margaret Atwood, "Fiction: Happy Endings"

Sentence-Composing Tools: Adverb Clause

DEFINITION

A dependent clause that gives more information about the rest of the sentence.
(For more about dependent clauses, see pages 68–73.) Like all clauses, adverb clauses contain a subject and its verb.

Adverb clauses answer these questions about an independent clause and begin with the words in parentheses (called *subordinate conjunctions*):

When does it happen? *(after, as, before, when, while, until)*
Why does it happen? *(because, since)*
How does it happen? *(as if, as though)*
Under what condition does it happen? *(although, if)*
Sentences can contain single or multiple adverb clauses:

Single Adverb Clauses:

1. **Although good looks may rally one's attention**, a lasting sense of a person's beauty reveals itself in stages.

   Diane Ackerman, "The Face of Beauty"

2. Delicatessens on Sunday night, **when all other stores are shut**, will overcharge you ferociously.

   Saul Bellow, "A Father-to-Be"

3. One leg was gone, and the other was held by tendons, and part of the trousers and stump twitched and jerked **as though it were not connected**.

   Ernest Hemingway, *A Farewell to Arms*

Multiple Adverb Clauses:

4. He was one of those guys that think they're being a pansy **if they don't break around forty of your fingers when they shake hands with you.** (*Contains two consecutive adverb clauses, one beginning with* if *and the other* when.)

   J. D. Salinger, *The Catcher in the Rye*

5. **When she grinned**, her baby teeth shone like a string of pearls, and **when she laughed**, her thin shoulders shook and twitched. (*Contains two nonconsecutive adverb clauses beginning with* when.)

   Keith Donohue, *The Stolen Child*

6. **As he soared upward, as the wind rushed through his hair, as the crowd's faces became mere flesh-colored pinpricks below,** and **as the Horntail shrank to the size of a dog,** he realized that he had left not only the ground behind, but also his fear. *(Contains four consecutive adverb clauses beginning with* as.*)*

J. K. Rowling, *Harry Potter and the Goblet of Fire*

Adverb clauses can be removed without destroying the basic meaning of the sentence, but notice how including them adds detail and style to the sentences. Adverb clauses build better sentences.

1a. A lasting sense of a person's beauty reveals itself in stages.

1b. **Although good looks may rally one's attention,** a lasting sense of a person's beauty reveals itself in stages.

2a. Delicatessens on Sunday night will overcharge you ferociously.

2b. Delicatessens on Sunday night, **when all other stores are shut,** will overcharge you ferociously.

3a. He realized that he had left not only the ground behind, but also his fear.

3b. **As he soared upward, as the wind rushed through his hair, as the crowd's faces became mere flesh-colored pinpricks below,** and **as the Horntail shrank to the size of a dog,** he realized that he had left not only the ground behind, but also his fear.

Using the Sentence-Composing Toolbox

PRACTICE 1: MATCHING

Match the adverb clauses with the sentences. Write out each sentence, inserting and underlining the adverb clauses.

Sentences:

1. The twins were enchanted by the sound of my voice and began at once to coo and clap their chubby hands ^.

   Keith Donohue, *The Stolen Child*

2. ^, at twenty-nine Tommy Castelli's life was a screaming bore.

   Bernard Malamud, "The Prison"

3. The drops of blood from the injured soldier fell very slowly, ^.

   Ernest Hemingway, *A Farewell to Arms*

4. The Buffalo Bar sounded like a terrible place, but ^, it seemed pretty nice.

   John Steinbeck, "Johnny Bear"

5. To my right is Gretchen, who's got her chin jutting out ^.

   Toni Cade Bambara, "Raymond's Run"

Adverb Clauses:

a. as if it would win the race all by it-self

b. when you walked down the night street, over the wooden sidewalks, when the long streamers of swamp fog, like waving, dirty bunting, flapped in your face, when finally you pushed open the swing doors and saw men sitting around talking and drinking, and Fat Carl coming along toward you

c. while long strings of drool ran down their chins

d. as they fall from an icicle after the sun has gone

e. although he tried not to think of it

PRACTICE 2: UNSCRAMBLING TO IMITATE

In the model and the scrambled list, identify the adverb clause. Next, unscramble and write out the sentence parts to imitate the model. Finally, write your own imitation of the model and identify the adverb clause.

MODEL: Because the railroads published schedules, the country was divided into four time zones.

Stephen E. Ambrose, *Nothing Like It in the World*

a. was covered

b. by shimmering light dew

c. before the sun came up

d. the grass

PRACTICE 3: COMBINING TO IMITATE

In the model, identify the adverb clause. Next, combine the list of sentences to imitate the model. Finally, write your own imitation of the model and identify the adverb clause.

MODEL: Since most of the silk available came from underclothing and evening dresses, the quilt they made was glorious in strips of flesh pink and orchid and pale yellow and cerise.

John Steinbeck, *Cannery Row*

a. It happened although many of the buttons were from discarded coats and worn-out blouses.

b. What happened was that the collage they created was diverse.

c. It was diverse in dabs of bright colors and pastels and gleaming silver and gold.

PRACTICE 4: IMITATING

Identify the adverb clauses in the models and sample imitations. Then write an imitation of each model sentence, one sentence part at a time. Read one of your imitations to see if your classmates can guess which model you imitated.

Models:

1. Although the villagers had forgotten the ritual and lost the original black box, they still remembered to use stones.

Shirley Jackson, "The Lottery"

Sample: Because the coach had chosen the team and wanted the most prestigious win, she always planned to be victorious.

2. The dog pranced round us, and then, before anyone could stop it, it made a dash for the condemned prisoner and, jumping up, tried to lick his face.

George Orwell, "A Hanging"

Sample: The toddler crawled toward her father, and then, while everyone was watching her, she made a lunge toward her beaming father, and, smiling brightly, began to say his name.

3. He had an aunt in Winesburg, a black-toothed old woman who raised chickens, and with her he lived until she died.

Sherwood Anderson, *Winesburg, Ohio*

Sample: No one liked the head of the company, a thrice-divorced drill sergeant who threatened everyone, and about him the employees gossiped until he appeared.

PRACTICE 5: EXPANDING

The adverb clauses are omitted at the caret mark (^) in the following sentences. For each caret, add an adverb clause, blending your content and style with the rest of the sentence.

1. While ^, I watched the mirror closely and became aware of my skull, of the fact that my teeth were rooted in bone, and that my jawbones and all the other bones lay just under the surface of what I could see.

Barbara Kingsolver, *Animal Dreams*

2. On stormy nights, when ^, the bay, fifty feet below the house, resembled an immense black pit, from which arose mutterings and sighs as if ^.

Joseph Conrad, "The Idiots"

3. During the whole of a dull, dark, and soundless day in the autumn of the year, when ^, I had been passing alone, on horseback, through a singularly dreary tract of country, and at length found myself, as ^, within view of the melancholy House of Usher.

Edgar Allan Poe, "The Fall of the House of Usher"

Sentence-Composing Tools: Noun Clause

DEFINITION

A dependent clause that works like a noun. (For more about dependent clauses, see pages 68–73.) Like all clauses, noun clauses contain a subject and its verb. To understand how noun clauses act like nouns, insert *what we eat for breakfast* into any of these blanks:

1. _____ is important. *(subject)*

2. We discussed _____. *(direct object)*

3. The health teacher talked about _____. *(object of preposition)*

4. A valuable part of a healthy diet is _____. *(predicate noun)*

5. A regular morning meal, _____, provides energy for school. *(appositive)*

Most noun clauses begin with *that, what,* or *how.* However, some noun clauses begin with other words. The best way to identify a noun clause is this: if a clause is removable, it's not a noun clause; if a clause is *not* removable, it is a noun clause.

Removable (Adverb or Adjective Clauses):

1. The exact year **when George Washington was born** was 1732. *(adjective clause)*

2. **When George Washington was born,** cars didn't exist. *(adverb clause)*

Nonremovable (Noun Clauses):

3 **When George Washington was born** was a question on the quiz.

4. The discussion was about **when George Washington was born.**

5. Mr. Jameson discussed **when George Washington was born.**

Sentences can contain single or multiple noun clauses:

Single Noun Clause:

1. The most insidious thing about Ronnie was **that weak minds found him worth imitating.**

> Stephen King, *Hearts in Atlantis*

2. Her mind only vaguely grasped **what he was saying.**

> Kate Chopin, "A Respectable Woman"

3. I don't know **how he found his way back to the car**.

> Annie Dillard, *An American Childhood*

Multiple Noun Clauses:

4. The writer must learn to read critically but constructively, to cut **what is bad**, to reveal **what is good**.

> Donald M. Murray, "The Maker's Eye: Revising Your Own Manuscripts"

5. Most of **what I write**, like most of **what I say in casual conversation**, will not amount to much.

> William Stafford, "A Way of Writing"

6. I asked him once **why he had to go away, why the land was so important**.

> Mildred D. Taylor, *Roll of Thunder, Hear My Cry*

PRACTICE 1: MATCHING

Match the noun clauses with the sentences. Write out each sentence, inserting and underlining the noun clauses.

Sentences:

1. Survivors still wonder ^.

   John Hersey, *Hiroshima*

2. He looked over to ^, their naked heads sunk in the hunched feathers.

   Ernest Hemingway, "The Snows of Kilimanjaro"

3. It was April and sunny outside, and I wondered ^.

   Frank McCourt, *Teacher Man*

4. ^ trickled thinly down his wrist.

   J. D. Salinger, "The Laughing Man"

5. Robert's mother declared ^.

   Tracy Kidder, *Among Schoolchildren*

Noun Clauses:

a. what little blood he had left

b. that Robert had his father's crazy genes

c. why they lived when so many others died

d. where the huge, filthy buzzards sat

e. how many Aprils I had left, how many sunny days

PRACTICE 2: UNSCRAMBLING TO IMITATE

In the model and the scrambled list, identify the noun clause. Next, unscramble and write out the sentence parts to imitate the model. Finally, write your own imitation of the model and identify the noun clause.

MODEL: He realized that the swollen flesh on the side of his mouth was a leech, growing fat as it sucked his lips.

> Michael Crichton, *Jurassic Park*

a. that the thin boy in the back of the room

b. taking notes as he concealed his intent

c. no one noticed

d. was an infiltrator

PRACTICE 3: COMBINING TO IMITATE

In the model, identify the noun clause. Next, combine the list of sentences to imitate the model. Finally, write your own imitation of the model and identify the noun clause.

MODEL: Not daring to glance at the books, I went out of the library, fearing that the librarian would call me back for further questioning.

> Richard Wright, *Black Boy*

a. He was not wanting to appear as a coward.

b. He dived down from the cliff.

c. He was hoping that his buddies would accept him soon.

d. He was hoping for acceptance into their fraternity.

PRACTICE 4: IMITATING

Identify the noun clauses in the models and sample imitations. Then write an imitation of each model sentence, one sentence part at a time. Read one of your imitations to see if your classmates can guess which model you imitated.

Models:

1. Others remembered that Phil Latham, the wrestling coach, lived just across the Common and that he was an expert in first aid.

John Knowles, A Separate Peace

Sample: No one knew that Sally Henderson, the winning student, sang Saturday nights at the nursing home and that she was a soprano of great talent.

2. When I pointed out that writing was such a slow process that it made me impatient with my poor handwriting, he suggested that I learn to type.

Daniel Keyes, Flowers for Algernon

Sample: When I asked why tennis was such a frustrating sport that it made me discontent with my low control, she suggested that I take up Ping-Pong.

3. Because of the routines we follow, we often forget that life is an ongoing adventure.

Maya Angelou, Wouldn't Take Nothing for My Journey Now

Sample: Because of the people we know, we always realize that friendship is the greatest treasure.

PRACTICE 5: EXPANDING

The noun clauses are omitted at the caret mark (^) in the following sentences. For each caret, add a noun clause, blending your content and style with the rest of the sentence.

1. What matters is what ^, not how ^.

Isabel Allende, Daughter of Fortune

2. They felt that ^, that ^.

John Steinbeck, The Red Pony

3. I could never tell the students in my classes how ^, how ^, how ^, how ^.

Frank McCourt, Teacher Man

REVIEWING THE TOOLS: ERNEST HEMINGWAY'S *THE OLD MAN AND THE SEA* ———

Directions: Using these abbreviations, identify the underlined tools. If you need to review the tool, study the pages below.

Clauses	Review These Pages
independent clause = INDC	68–73
adjective clause = ADJC	74–78
adverb clause = ADVC	80–84
noun clause = NC	86–89

REVIEW 1: IDENTIFYING ————————————————————————

Directions: Write the abbreviation of the underlined tool.

1. Then the old fisherman looked behind him and saw <u>that no land was visible</u>.

2. The shark still hung to the marlin with his jaws hooked, and <u>the old man stabbed him in his left eye</u>.

3. He was a very big Mako shark, <u>which is built to swim as fast as the fastest fish in the sea</u>, and everything about him was beautiful except his jaws.

4. Just then the fish gave a sudden lurch that pulled the old man down onto the bow and would have pulled him overboard <u>if he had not braced himself and given some line</u>.

5. Up the road, in his shack, <u>the old man was sleeping again</u>.

6. The boy had given him two fresh small tunas, or albacores, <u>which hung on the two deepest lines like plummets</u>.

7. The old man looked ahead and saw a flight of wild ducks etching themselves against the sky over the water, then blurring, then etching again, and he knew <u>that no man was ever alone on the sea</u>.

8. The two sharks closed together, and <u>as he saw the one nearest him open its jaws and sink them into the silver side of his fish</u>, he raised the club high and brought it down heavy and slamming onto the top of the shark's broad head.

Directions: Write the abbreviation of each underlined tool. Each sentence illustrates a combination of tools from the four tools listed.

Example:

Sentence: (A) <u>Once there had been a tinted photograph of his wife on the wall</u>, but (B) <u>he took it down</u> (C) <u>because it made him too lonely to see it</u>, and (D) <u>it was on the shelf in the corner under his clean shirt</u>.

Answers:

    (A)—INDC (independent clause)   (C)—ADVC (adverb clause)

    (B)—INDC (independent clause)   (D)—INDC (independent clause)

9. The shark let go of the fish and slid down, swallowing (A) <u>what he had taken</u> (B) <u>as he died</u>.

10. (A) <u>If there is a hurricane</u>, (B) <u>you always see the signs of it in the sky for days ahead</u>, (C) <u>if you are at sea</u>.

11. Some of the younger fishermen, (A) <u>who used buoys as floats for their lines and had motorboats</u>, bought (B) <u>when the shark livers brought much money</u>, spoke of the sea as *la mar*, (C) <u>which is feminine</u>.

12. (A) <u>When the old man saw the shark coming</u>, he knew (B) <u>that this was a shark that had no fear at all and would do exactly</u> (C) <u>what it wished</u>.

13. (A) <u>When the old man gaffed the female marlin and clubbed her and hoisted her aboard</u>, holding the rapier bill with its sandpaper edge and clubbing her across the top of her head (B) <u>until her colour turned to a colour almost like the backing of mirrors</u>, (C) <u>the male marlin stayed by the side of the boat</u>.

14. (A) <u>The marlin's sword was as long as a baseball bat and tapered like a rapier</u>, and (B) <u>the fish rose his full length from the water and then re-entered it</u>, smoothly, like a diver, and (C) <u>the old man saw the great scythe-blade of his tail go under</u>, and (D) <u>the line commenced to go out</u>.

15. (A) <u>These sharks would cut the turtles' legs and flippers off</u> (B) <u>when the turtles were asleep on the sea's surface</u>, and (C) <u>they would hit a man in the water</u> (D) <u>if they were hungry</u>, even (E) <u>if the man had no smell of fish blood nor of fish slime on him</u>.

REVIEW 2: IMITATING

The following model sentences contain the four tools you just reviewed—independent clauses, adjective clauses, adverb clauses, and noun clauses—as well as other kinds of sentence-composing tools. For each model sentence, write the letter of its imitation. Then write your own imitation of the same model.

Using the Sentence-Composing Toolbox

Model Sentences:

1. They were hateful sharks, bad smelling, scavengers as well as killers, and when they were hungry, they would bite at an oar or the rudder of a boat.

2. He had sailed for two hours, resting in the stern and sometimes chewing a bit of the meat from the marlin, trying to rest and to be strong, when he saw the first of the two sharks.

3. Many fishermen were around the skiff looking at what was lashed beside it, and one was in the water, his trousers rolled up, measuring the marlin's skeleton with a length of line.

4. The old man no longer dreamed of storms, nor of women, nor of great occurrences, nor of great fish, nor fights, nor contests of strength, nor of his wife, but dreamed now only of places and of the lions on the beach.

5. Those who caught sharks took them to the shark factory on the other side of the cove, where they were hoisted on a block and tackle, their livers removed, their fins cut off, their hides skinned out, and their flesh cut into strips for salting.

Imitations:

A. Many fans were near the stage, rocking to what was played in the encore, and most were on their feet, their hands raised up, yelling the song's lyrics with a frenzy of energy.

B. Those who loved novels took them to their private rooms in the dormitory section of the campus, where pages were marked with pens or highlighters, their plots analyzed, their themes explored, their characters analyzed, and their paragraphs reduced to sentences for studying.

C. They were beautiful dancers, young looking, ballerinas as well as gymnasts, and when the curtain went up, they would take charge of the stage for the audience at each performance.

D. The losing quarterback no longer thought of games, nor of victory, nor of long runs, nor of great blocks, nor tackles, nor banquets of celebration, nor of his team, but thought now only of his loss of respect in the school.

E. He had waited in intense concentration, thinking about the argument and sometimes remembering a line of her accusation from their disagreement, hoping to forgive and to be forgiven, when he heard the sound of the opening front door.

REVIEW 3: CREATING

In Ernest Hemingway's novel *The Old Man and the Sea*, Santiago, the main character who earns his living as a fisherman, has caught no fish for eighty-four days. Undaunted, he takes his skiff out to sea, and catches the biggest marlin he has ever caught.

When Santiago was even with the marlin and had the fish's head against the bow of the skiff, he could not believe his size. "He is my fortune," he thought. The marlin was so big it was like lashing a much bigger skiff alongside. The old man looked at the fish constantly.

It was an hour before the first shark hit him.

"The Shark Attack" below is based on Santiago's strenuous battle with the shark that attacks his marlin.

At the caret (^), use your imagination to add clauses—independent, adjective, adverb, and noun—to make the paragraph good enough to appear in the original novel!

"The Shark Attack"

(1) The shark, which ^, caught the scent of blood from the marlin lashed to the old man's skiff. (2) When ^, the shark broke through the surface of the water, rose above it in the sun, and fell back into it, following the blood trail. (3) The old man knew what ^ but hoped that ^. (4) As ^, the old man prepared to fight the shark, grabbing his harpoon, which ^. (5) Suddenly, after ^, the shark attacked the marlin, its jaws wide for the attack and teeth like sharp razors biting into the fish. (6) ^, and the old man with all his strength drove his harpoon deep into the shark's head.

PREVIEW

In the following sections of *Grammar for High School: A Sentence-Composing Approach*, you'll learn how the best writers of our times vary the use of the fourteen tools you've just mastered.

One variation is to include multiple tools of the same kind within a single sentence. Another variation is to use a combination of different kinds of tools within a single sentence.

Also, you'll learn and practice how those writers use special punctuation marks—colons, semicolons, dashes—to make their sentences more effective.

At the end of the worktext, you'll study, analyze, and imitate all the sentence-composing tools in all their varieties and special punctuation marks in the writing of William Golding, author of the novel *Lord of the Flies*.

Finally, for the last activity of *Grammar for High School: A Sentence-Composing Approach*, using "the grammar of the greats," you'll write an original episode for a sequel to *Lord of the Flies*, so well written that it would perhaps be worthy of publication.

A writer is not someone who expresses thoughts, passion or imagination in sentences but someone who thinks sentences. A Sentence-Thinker.

—Roland Barthes, professional writer

Think sentences!

Any tool can be multiplied by putting two or more of the same kind of tool next to each other, separated by commas. Multiplying tools is common in the sentences of authors.

Positions:

Opener (before a subject and its verb): **Taking what might have been measured as a halting half step** and then **pulling a stiff, dead leg forward, dragging a foot turned sideways in the dust**, the man limped into the yard. *(tools: multiple present participial phrases)*

William H. Armstrong, Sounder

S-V split (between a subject and its verb): Little Man, **a very small six-year-old** and **a most finicky dresser**, was brushing his hair when I entered. *(tools: multiple appositive phrases)*

Mildred D. Taylor, Roll of Thunder, Hear My Cry

Closer (after a subject and its verb): Bobby walked slowly toward his bedroom door, **his head down** and **his eyes on the toes of his sneakers**. *(tools: multiple absolute phrases)*

Stephen King, Hearts in Atlantis

In the following practices, you will be working with all fourteen of the sentence-composing tools covered earlier in this worktext. To review any of them, study the pages indicated. Sentences are from the Harry Potter novels by J. K. Rowling.

The Sentence-Composing Tools

Words:

1. *Opening adjective (pages 14–17):* **Furious**, Harry threw his ingredients and his bag into his cauldron and dragged it up to the front of the dungeon to the empty table.

Harry Potter and the Goblet of Fire

2. *Delayed adjective (pages 18–21):* Harry was on his feet again, **furious, ready to fly at Dumbledore**, who had plainly not understood Sirius at all.

Harry Potter and the Order of the Phoenix

3. *Opening adverb (pages 22–25):* **Slowly, very slowly**, the snake raised its head until its eyes were on a level with Harry's.

   Harry Potter and the Sorcerer's Stone

4. *Delayed adverb (pages 26–29):* The gigantic snake was nearing Frank, and then, **incredibly, miraculously**, it passed him, following the spitting, hissing noises made by the cold voice beyond the door.

   Harry Potter and the Goblet of Fire

Phrases:

5. *Absolute (pages 34–38):* Soon, the crowd of gnomes in the field started walking away in a staggering line, **their little shoulders hunched**.

   Harry Potter and the Chamber of Secrets

6. *Appositive (pages 40–43):* Fudge, **a portly little man in a long, pinstriped cloak**, looked cold and exhausted.

   Harry Potter and the Prisoner of Azkaban

7. *Prepositional (pages 44–47):* **At daybreak on a fine summer's morning**, when the Riddle House had still been well kept and impressive, a maid had entered the drawing room to find all three Riddles dead.

   Harry Potter and the Chamber of Secrets

8. *Participial (pages 48–52):* **Hating himself, repulsed by what he was doing**, Harry forced the goblet back toward Dumbledore's mouth and tipped it for Dumbledore to drink the remainder of the horrible potion inside. *(Note: Contains both present and past participial phrases.)*

   Harry Potter and the Half-Blood Prince

9. *Gerund (pages 54–57):* **Conjuring up portable, waterproof fires** was a specialty of Hermione's.

   Harry Potter and the Chamber of Secrets

10. *Infinitive (pages 58–62):* **To make Dudley feel better about eating "rabbit food,"** Aunt Petunia had insisted that the whole family follow the same diet, too.

    Harry Potter and the Goblet of Fire

Clauses:

11. *Independent clause (pages 68–73):* **He raised the wand above his head and brought it swishing down through the dusty air** as a stream of red and gold sparks shot from the end like a firework, throwing dancing spots of light onto the walls. *(See also sentence 13 below.)*

    Harry Potter and the Sorcerer's Stone

12. *Adjective clause (pages 74–78):* The first thing they saw was Peeves the Poltergeist, **who was floating upside down in midair and stuffing the nearest keyhole with chewing gum**.

    Harry Potter and the Prisoner of Azkaban

13. *Adverb clause (pages 80–84):* He raised the wand above his head and brought it swishing down through the dusty air **as a stream of red and gold sparks shot from the end like a firework**, throwing dancing spots of light onto the walls. *(See also sentence 11 above.)*

    Harry Potter and the Sorcerer's Stone

14. *Noun clause (pages 86–89):* Harry knew **that Dumbledore was going to refuse, that he would tell Riddle there would be plenty of time for practical demonstrations at Hogwarts**, and **that they were currently in a building full of Muggles and must therefore be cautious**.

    Harry Potter and the Half-Blood Prince

PRACTICE 1: MATCHING

Match the multiple tools with their sentences. Write out each sentence, inserting the multiple tools at the caret (^) and underlining them. Name the multiplied tool; there is one example for each of the fourteen tools listed.

Part One—Sentences:

1. ^, the water had turned into an ugly, angered river.

   Bill and Vera Cleaver,
   Where the Lilies Bloom

Part One—Multiple Tools:

a. what was done by the iceberg and what was caused by the impact as the ship struck the ocean floor

2. She looked neither right nor left, ^.
   Robert Lipsyte, *The Contender*

b. reheating coffee, making popcorn, and putting some heat on take-out from places like Cluck-Cluck Tonite

3. The true nature of the damage to the *Titanic* may be partly revealed as exploration of the wreck continues over the coming years, but it will often be hard to tell ^.
   Walter Lord, *The Night Lives On*

c. her eyes focusing straight ahead, her face glowing with the quiet joys of Sunday

4. ^, spring enveloped all of us.
   Mildred D. Taylor, *Roll of Thunder, Hear My Cry*

d. to his home, to his comfort, to the bringing up of their children, to the garden and her greenhouse, to the local church, and to her patchwork quilts

5. ^, Margaret had happily given her life.
   P. D. James, *A Certain Justice*

e. rain-drenched, fresh, vital, full of life

6. ^, they walked, but the view did not vary.
   J. K. Rowling, *Harry Potter and the Half-Blood Prince*

f. belching dirt and stones, and carrying blown branches along in its torrent

7. He believed the only three valid purposes microwaves served were ^.
   Stephen King, *Needful Things*

g. on and on

Part Two—Sentences:

8. With a gentle forefinger, he stroked the turtle's throat and chest ^.

   John Steinbeck, *The Red Pony*

9. She failed to see a shadow, ^.

   Gaston Leroux, *The Phantom of the Opera*

10. In New York, ^, Democrats were joyous and Republicans angry and gloomy.

    John F. Kennedy, *Profiles in Courage*

11. If Sam had looked back, he might have seen not far below Gollum turn again, and then with a wild light of madness glaring in his eyes come, ^, creeping on behind, a slinking shadow among the stones.

    J. R. R. Tolkien, *The Lord of the Rings*

12. A voice suddenly shouted at me, ^, although I couldn't understand the words.

    Robert Cormier, *Take Me Where the Good Times Are*

13. The monster dinosaur twitched its jeweler's hands down ^.

    Ray Bradbury, "A Sound of Thunder"

14. The blood no longer pulsed, but ^.

    Ann Patchett, *Bel Canto*

Part Two—Multiple Tools:

h. swiftly but warily

i. the most important state in any Presidential race, and a state where politics were particularly sensitive to the views of various nationality and minority groups

j. it continued to seep, and Messner stopped to blot it away with a napkin

k. loud and strong and angry

l. which followed her like her own shadow, which stopped when she stopped, and which started again when she did

m. to fondle the men, to twist them in half, to crush them like berries, to cram them into its teeth and its screaming throat

n. until the turtle relaxed, until its eyes closed and it lay languorous and asleep

PRACTICE 2: UNSCRAMBLING TO IMITATE

In the model and the scrambled list, identify the multiple tool. Next, unscramble and write out the sentence parts to imitate the model. Finally, write your own imitation of the model and identify the multiple tool.

1. MODEL: **When the first heavy rains were falling** and **as a cold wind whistled through the valley**, a knock came at the minister's door.

    Louisa May Alcott, "Onawandah"

    a. before the first scrimmage was played
    b. the team rallied
    c. despite the outcome
    d. and after the last game ended in defeat

2. MODEL: **Dizzy** and **sick to his stomach**, he felt as if the whole car were moving beneath him.

    Michael Crichton, *Jurassic Park*

    a. were falling on her
    b. hysterical and down on her knees
    c. as though the plaster ceiling
    d. Matilda crumbled

3. MODEL: Janet and the Tiger went racing back, **over the country** and **over the town, over houses and churches and mountains and rivers, across the park** and **along the street**, and **in Janet's window**.

    Joan Aiken, "A Necklace of Raindrops"

    a. and into the mermaid's home
    b. amid fish and whales and sharks and jellyfish
    c. under the swimmers and under the boat
    d. the mermaid and the dolphin
    e. across the lagoon and below the surface
    f. went diving down

4. MODEL: **A little corn was raised on the sterile slope**, and **it grew short and thick under the wind**, and **all the cobs formed on the landward sides of the stalks**.

    John Steinbeck, "Flight"

   a. so each of the blossoms
   b. a few daffodils
   c. but they looked dwarfed and timid beside the tree
   d. were coming up in the back garden
   e. strained toward the sunny side of the garden

5. MODEL: **Clapping** and **stepping in unison**, our group moved away from the swarms, which thrummed deeply and followed.

Michael Crichton, Prey

   a. which screeched loudly
   b. laughing
   c. her brother yelled into the microphone
   d. and singing off key
   e. and died

6. MODEL: **Instantly, obediently**, Jonas dropped his bike on its side on the path behind his family's dwelling.

Lois Lowry, The Giver

   a. Carrie threw her books
   b. spitefully
   c. of her roommate's messy area
   d. intentionally
   e. on the desk in the corner

7. MODEL: His parents furnished the house by **taking his grandparents' few pieces from storage** and **buying what else they needed from the cheaper London auction houses**.

P. D. James, A Certain Justice

   a. controlled his nerves
   b. from a fearful unsteady board approach
   c. and realizing what he stood to lose
   d. the semifinalist
   e. by taking several deep breaths before the dive

PRACTICE 3: IMITATING

Identify the multiple tools within the models and sample imitations. Then write an imitation of each model, one sentence part at a time. Read one of your imitations to see if your classmates can guess which model you imitated.

Models:

1. She forgot even her sorrow at the sharp report of his gun and the piteous sight of thrushes and sparrows dropping silent to the ground, **their songs hushed** and **their pretty feathers stained and wet with blood**.

    Sarah Orne Jewett, "A White Heron"

    Sample: Ricka thought about her future at the start of the processional music and the poignant sight of young men and young women streaming quietly across the stage, their faces flushed and their graduation gowns ironed but damp with perspiration.

2. She turned and looked in the other direction, up toward Cold Mountain, **pale** and **gray** and **distant**, then down into Black Cove.

    Charles Frazier, *Cold Mountain*

    Sample: He stood and glanced from the waiting building, down toward the traffic, dense and sluggish and loud, then up into the blue sky.

3. Tim wanted **to bend down, to look below the table at the raptor**, but he didn't dare move.

    Michael Crichton, *Jurassic Park*

    Sample: Helen wanted to disappear quietly, to melt into the crowd in the terminal, but she couldn't quite manage.

4. Kirsti had gone to bed reluctantly, complaining **that she wanted to stay up with the others, that she was grown-up enough, that she had never before seen a dead person in a closed-up box, that it wasn't *fair***.

    Lois Lowry, *Number the Stars*

    Sample: Susan had cried herself to sleep eventually, wondering how she made her friends hate her, how she had ruined everything, how she had never before yelled at friends in a sudden rage, how she was not herself.

5. In his room on the ground floor, to the right of the front door, Father Kleinsorge changed into a military uniform, **which he had acquired when he was teaching at the Rokko Middle School in Kobe** and **which he wore during air-raid alerts**.

    John Hersey, *Hiroshima*

Sample: In his locker in the boys' locker room, at the end of the bank of lockers, Corey took out his baseball mitt, which his father gave him when Corey started playing seriously at the age of thirteen and which he counted on during any championship game.

6. The dawn came quickly now, **a wash, a glow, a lightness**, and then **an explosion of fire**, as the sun arose out of the Gulf.

     John Steinbeck, *The Pearl*

Sample: The pill melted slowly then, a fizz, a clump, a circle, and then an absence of color, as the ingredients disappeared completely into the water.

7. He spoke on, **firmly** and **clearly**, with such joyful enthusiasm that Eilonwy had no heart to stop him.

     Lloyd Alexander, *The High King*

Sample: Aminata dashed onward, quickly and steadily, with such practiced skill that no one doubted her ability to outrace Janet.

PRACTICE 4: EXPANDING

Multiple tools are omitted at the caret mark (^) in the following sentences. For each caret, add the tool indicated, blending your content and style with the rest of the sentence.

1. *Opening adjectives:* ^ and ^, he looked as if he had slept in his clothes, and in fact he often did, after a marathon programming session.

     Michael Crichton, *Prey*

2. *Delayed adjectives:* He was an elderly man, ^ and ^.

     Gregory David Roberts, *Shantaram*

3. *Opening adverbs:* ^, ^, ^, the melody of the morning, the music of evil, of the enemy sounded, but it was faint and weak.

     John Steinbeck, *The Pearl*

4. *Delayed adverbs:* Griffin was light and fast, his gloves a red blur tapping away at Alfred's face, ^ and ^.

     Robert Lipsyte, *The Contender*

5. *Absolute phrases:* Mr. Barnett, his ^ and his ^, immediately pounced on her.

Mildred D. Taylor, *Roll of Thunder, Hear My Cry*

6. *Appositive phrases:* There they all were now, the ^, the ^, with their high I.Q.'s and expensive shoes, pasting each other with snowballs.

John Knowles, *A Separate Peace*

7. *Prepositional phrases:* Then they came, up ^ and around ^.

Hal Borland, *When the Legends Die*

8. *Participial phrases:* What she remembered was Emmanuel, ^, ^, ^, as they walked tardily home from school.

Gwendolyn Brooks, "Helen"

9. *Gerund phrases:* There were sounds of ^ and ^, and a moment later he appeared, his hands full of tops and marbles and old dusty kites and junk collected through the years.

Ray Bradbury, *The Martian Chronicles*

10. *Infinitive phrases:* Slowly, I crawled on, stopping to ^, to ^, to ^.

Scott O'Dell, *Island of the Blue Dolphins*

11. *Independent clauses:* A laugh trembled at his lips, but ^, so ^.

Evan Connell Jr., "The Condor and the Guests"

12. *Adjective clauses:* I saw that my old friend, who ^, who ^, who ^, was crying a little bit.

Stephen King, *Hearts in Atlantis*

13. *Adverb clauses:* Inman fired his rifle until ^, until ^.

Charles Frazier, *Cold Mountain*

14. *Noun clauses:* My first draft of my writing usually has only a few elements worth keeping, and I have to find out what ^ and build from them and throw out what ^, or what ^.

Susan Sontag (quotation)

Multiplying the Tools

CREATIVE WRITING

Composing a paragraph—Pretend that you are one of the following authors who has written the first sentence of a long story. Choose one of the sentences listed as the first sentence in a paragraph that will begin that story. Create the rest of the paragraph.

Just as the writers' sentences use multiple tools, within your paragraph use multiple tools and other sentence-composing tools you've learned to make your paragraph memorable.

Reminder: Don't try to write a complete story. Write, revise, and finalize only the first paragraph of that story. (Maybe later you'll want to write the entire story!)

1. He walked with his blazer clasped **by a finger over his shoulder, across the Common, through the Public Garden, over the bridges and along the curving paths that rim the lagoon**. *(multiple prepositional phrases)*

   Jhumpa Lahiri, *The Namesake*

2. Miss Pennington walked among them, **tall** and **willowy**, pausing first at this desk and then at that one to answer questions. *(multiple delayed adjectives)*

   Anne Tyler, *Saint Maybe*

3. A tall boy with glittering golden hair and a sulky mouth pushed and jostled a light wheel chair along, in which sat a small weary dying man, **his weak dark whiskers flecked with gray, his spread hands limp on the brown blanket over his knees, eyes closed**. *(multiple absolute phrases)*

   Katherine Anne Porter, *Ship of Fools*

4. The park had the usual attractions, **a boardwalk, a Ferris wheel, roller coasters, bumper cars, a taffy stand**, and **an arcade where you could shoot streams of water into a clown's mouth**. *(multiple appositive phrases)*

   Mitch Albom, *The Five People You Meet in Heaven*

5. It was an eccentric, rainy, wind-beaten sea village, **downtrodden** and **mildewed, the boards of its buildings bleached and weathered, their drainpipes rusted a dull orange**. *(multiple past participial phrases and multiple absolute phrases)*

   David Guterson, *Snow Falling on Cedars*

Tip for Better Revising: Always, when you revise something you've written, look for places to use multiple tools plus other sentence-composing tools to add detail, interest, and style to your writing.

Effective writers sometimes add detail to their sentences by mixing two or more different tools within the same sentence.

Most authors use a mix of tools frequently, placing sentence-composing tools within these positions: opener, S-V split, closer, and two or more of those positions.

Positions:

Opener mix (before a subject and its verb): **Scrawny, blue-lipped, the skin around his eyes and the corners of his mouth a dark exploded purple**, he looked like something an archeologist might find in the burial room of a pyramid. *(opening adjective, past participle, absolute phrase)*

Stephen King, Bag of Bones

S-V split mix (between a subject and its verb): Huston, **a tall spare man, wind-blackened, with eyes like little blades**, spoke to his committee. *(appositive phrase, past participial phrase, prepositional phrases)*

John Steinbeck, The Grapes of Wrath

Closer mix (after a subject and its verb): Seabiscuit's jockey Red Pollard was an elegant young man, **tautly muscled, with a shock of supernaturally orange hair.** *(past participial phrase, prepositional phrases)*

Laura Hillenbrand, Seabiscuit

Other mix (two or more different positions): **There, placed on one of the hooks above the woodbox**, was my high-school jacket, **the one with the big white GF entwined on the breast**. *(**opener:** opening adverb, past participial phrase; **closer:** appositive phrase)*

Stephen King, Hearts in Atlantis

Opener Mix

DEFINITION

Two or more different tools at the beginning of a sentence. Mixing two or more different writer's tools within the opener position is common in professional writing. The tools can be any mix of the tools covered in this worktext.

Examples:

1. **Finally, near dawn**, Eliza stopped bleeding. *(opening adverb, prepositional phrase)*

   Isabel Allende, *Daughter of Fortune*

2. **Stunned, gasping**, Mafatu raised his head and looked about. *(past participle, present participle)*

   Armstrong Sperry, *Call It Courage*

3. **Unlike her son Doc, who was easygoing**, Mother Smith was a thin feisty little woman who had been quite a beauty when she was younger. *(prepositional phrase, adjective clause)*

   Fannie Flagg, *Standing in the Rainbow*

4. **Concerned with her father, who lay dying in the bedroom, but not wanting to miss the moon landing**, Phyllis was with her father when her mother called her to come and see Neil Armstrong set foot on the moon. *(past participial phrase, adjective clause, present participial phrase)*

   Frank McCourt, *Teacher Man*

PRACTICE 1: MATCHING

Match the mixed tools with their sentences. Write out each sentence, inserting the tools at the caret (^) marks and underlining them. Name the tools.

Sentences:

1. ^, the black shapes became terribly clear.

   J. R. R. Tolkien, *Lord of the Rings: The Fellowship of the Ring*

Opener Mixes:

a. Above the smoke-blackened fortress and the burial mound, whose fresh earth was already frost-covered

2. ^, I stood, in love and at ease and always young, on the packed lower deck.

    Dylan Thomas, "Quite Early One Morning"

3. ^, the clouds had grown heavy.

    Lloyd Alexander, *The High King*

4. ^, I would have attempted an agonizing reappraisal of my life.

    Frank McCourt, *Teacher Man*

5. ^, he surveyed the goings-on through a scrim of cynicism.

    Anne Tyler, *The Amateur Marriage*

b. Carefree, open-collared, my eyes alight, my veins full of the spring, as a dancer's shoes should be full of champagne

c. If I had any kind of intelligence, beyond mere sniffing survival skills

d. Immediately, although everything else remained as before, dim and dark

e. Slumped glumly on Anna's piano bench before the meal, arms folded, chin on his chest

PRACTICE 2: UNSCRAMBLING TO IMITATE

In the model and the scrambled list, identify the opener mix and name the tools within it. Next, unscramble and write out the sentence parts to imitate the model. Finally, write your own imitation of the model and identify the tools within the opener mix.

1. MODEL: **While she sat in the drawing room, feeling her tiredness at last but unwilling to go to bed**, her mother was questioned by the inspector.

    Ian McEwan, *Atonement*

    a. was frustrated by the deficit
    b. after the audit from the central office
    c. and trying to balance the books
    d. the accountant
    e. calculating the bottom line with care

2. MODEL: **In 1839, when the Opium War between China and Great Britain broke out**, Tao Chi'en was sixteen years old.

    Isabel Allende, *Daughter of Fortune*

    a. was the only fireman
    b. burst forth

c. Rory Calhoun
d. while the fireworks over the fairground and the audience
e. on July 4th

3. MODEL: **A very slow speaker, averaging hardly a hundred words a minute,** Webster combined the musical charm of his deep organ-like voice and a striking appearance to make his orations a magnet that drew crowds.

John F. Kennedy, Profiles in Courage

a. listening closely a small percentage of the time
b. and a whimsical smile
c. Jordan used the rich expressiveness of his pleasantly deceptive face
d. to create an appearance that charmed teachers
e. a mildly inattentive student

4. MODEL: **Jumping from the bed, my feet barely hitting the deerskin rug,** I rushed into Mama's room.

Mildred D. Taylor, Roll of Thunder, Hear My Cry

a. screamed
b. his hands barely grasping the shaky limb
c. hanging from the tree
d. with renewed vigor
e. Kowalski

5. MODEL: **Near the cab, parked in front of the mortuary,** was a huge Oldsmobile.

Stephen King, Hearts in Atlantis

a. was
b. under the bed
c. the secret puppy
d. wrapped in towels
e. from the bathroom

PRACTICE 3: IMITATING

Identify the tools within the opener position in the models and sample imitations. Then write an imitation of each model, one sentence part at a time. Read one of your imitations to see if your classmates can guess which model you imitated.

Models:

1. **Faintly,** but **with heart-rending distinctness,** the listeners could hear the sounds of weeping.

F. R. Buckley, "Gold-Mounted Guns"

Sample: Slowly, and **with careful attention,** the woodworker would carve the shapes of animals.

2. **Not daring to turn her head, from a corner of her eye,** she grew aware of a strange, humped shadow, motionless now.

Lloyd Alexander, *The High King*

Sample: Not wanting to draw anyone's attention, from a place in the back row, she became familiar with the slow, ballet move, graceful now.

3. **Twice, when the train lurched,** he sat up, looking around fiercely.

Robert Lipsyte, *The Contender*

Sample: Later, after the party ended, he wandered outside, walking around slowly.

4. **Suddenly, with shocking speed,** the fog cleared, the particles coalescing into two fully formed columns that now stood directly before us, rising and falling in dark ripples.

Michael Crichton, *Prey*

Sample: Furiously, with no warning, the rain began, the drops forming into thin silver sheets that now poured fiercely upon the village, striking and pounding upon the flimsy huts.

5. **Quiet, frightened,** and **wishing just to dump T. J. on his front porch and get back to the safety of our own beds,** we hastened along the invisible road, brightened only by the round light of the flashlight.

Mildred D. Taylor, *Roll of Thunder, Hear My Cry*

Sample: Nervous, excited, and **hoping simply to master the triple axle in his routine and continue skating with the confidence of his accumulated victories,** he wound around the glistening ice, focused completely on his approach to the upcoming crucial turn.

PRACTICE 4: EXPANDING

Below are sentences with the opener mix omitted. Add an opener mix of different tools at the caret mark (^), blending your content and style with the rest of the sentence.

1. ^, they returned to the car lot, exhausted and laughing, drinking beer from brown paper bags.

    Mitch Albom, *The Five People You Meet in Heaven*

2. ^, Tim was knocked flat on the seat, blinking in the darkness, his mouth warm with blood.

    Michael Crichton, *Jurassic Park*

3. ^, Joel Backman strutted out of the Rudley Federal Correctional Facility at five minutes after midnight, fourteen years ahead of schedule.

    John Grisham, *The Broker*

4. ^, she had noticed very soon one little girl, about her own age, who looked at her very hard with a pair of light, rather dull, blue eyes.

    Frances Hodgson Burnett, *A Little Princess*

5. ^, was a coffin-lid.

    Leo Tolstoy, "The Death of Ivan Ilych"

CREATIVE WRITING

Composing a paragraph—Pretend that you are one of the following authors who has written the first sentence of a long story. Choose one of the sentences listed as the first sentence in a paragraph that will begin that story. Create the rest of the paragraph.

Just as the writers' sentences use tools within an opener mix, within your paragraph use opener mixes and other sentence-composing tools you've learned to make your paragraph memorable.

Reminder: Don't try to write a complete story. Write, revise, and finalize only the first paragraph of that story. (Maybe later you'll want to write the entire story!)

1. **Beside the entrance way, looking at her with dark, unblinking eyes**, stood the biggest rat she had ever seen. *(prepositional phrase, present participial phrase)*

   Robert C. O'Brien, *Mrs. Frisby and the Rats of NIMH*

2. **To look at Richard, with his T-shirt and blue jeans, his hair down to his shoulders, a red bandanna wrapped pirate style around his head**, you might mistake him for a hippie. *(infinitive phrase, prepositional phrase, two absolute phrases)*

   Lee Stringer, *Grand Central Winter*

3. **Sitting in the truck, the windows down** and **the hot sun burning their arms**, they gnawed at the salty, overspiced chicken, huge crumbs falling. *(present participial phrase, two absolute phrases)*

   Annie Proulx, *Bad Dirt*

4. **Dry-mouthed, unaware that his eyes had filled with tears**, Bobby tore open the envelope, which was no bigger than the ones in which children send their first-grade valentines. *(past participial phrase, delayed adjective phrase)*

   Stephen King, *Hearts in Atlantis*

5. **Finally, near dawn**, Eliza stopped bleeding. *(opening adverb, prepositional phrase)*

   Isabel Allende, *Daughter of Fortune*

Tip for Better Revising: Always, when you revise something you've written, look for places to use a mixture of tools in the opening position plus other sentence-composing tools to add detail, interest, and style to your writing.

S-V Split Mix

DEFINITION

Two or more different tools between a subject and its verb. Mixing two or more different writer's tools within the S-V split position is common in professional writing. The tools can be any mixture of the tools covered in this worktext.

Examples:

1. Forty people, **dressed in black, somber,** nearly filled the little chapel. *(past participial phrase, delayed adjective)*

   Charles Frazier, *Cold Mountain*

2. Huston, **a tall spare man, wind-blackened, with eyes like little blades,** spoke to his committee, one man from each sanitary unit. *(appositive phrase, past participial phrase, prepositional phrase)*

   John Steinbeck, *The Grapes of Wrath*

3. The day, **like all days that are charged with a multiplicity of activity, physical** and **mental,** seemed to have lasted for more than the fifteen hours he had been working. *(prepositional phrase, delayed adjectives)*

   P. D. James, *A Certain Justice*

4. A month later, at about four o'clock in the afternoon, a dusty old four-door green Packard, **packed full of people, songbooks, and clothes, with sound equipment piled up on the top and on the running boards,** drove up to the Smith house. *(past participial phrase, prepositional phrase)*

   Fannie Flagg, *Standing in the Rainbow*

PRACTICE 1: MATCHING

Match the mixed tools with their sentences. Write out each sentence, inserting the tools at the caret (^) marks and underlining them. Name the tools.

Sentences:

1. The canoe, ^, twisted and shifted in the rushing waters.

   Armstrong Sperry, *Call It Courage*

S-V Split Mixes:

a. mortified and angered, vengeful

2. Ricky, ^, worked down at Sonny's Sunoco.

    Stephen King, *Needful Things*

    b. stripped of sail and mast, without a paddle to guide it in the swift-racing current

3. The rooster she wounded with the stick, ^, flew up on to her head and in fury clawed her hair.

    Bill and Vera Cleaver, *Where the Lilies Bloom*

    c. patched, frayed, and dirty

4. Every year, this aged old hat, ^, sorted new students into the four Hogwarts houses.

    J. K. Rowling, *Harry Potter and the Chamber of Secrets*

    d. nineteen, not overburdened with brains

5. The curtains, ^, were drawn, and seemed to reflect their cheerfulness throughout the room.

    Madeleine L'Engle, *A Wrinkle in Time*

    e. red, with a blue and green geometrical pattern

PRACTICE 2: UNSCRAMBLING TO IMITATE

In the model and the scrambled list, identify the S-V split mix and name the tools within it. Next, unscramble and write out the sentence parts to imitate the model. Finally, write your own imitation of the model and identify the tools within the S-V split mix.

1. MODEL: Marguerite Frolicher, **a young Swiss girl, accompanying her father on a business trip**, woke up with a memory of her bad dream.

    Walter Lord, *A Night to Remember*

    a. practiced with the determination
    b. a remarkable young quarterback
    c. leading his team to a championship season
    d. of a super athlete
    e. Stanley Kramer

2. MODEL: Ada, **a hand cupped to her mouth, leaning**, spoke softly to a man across the aisle from her.

> Charles Frazier, *Cold Mountain*

   a. crouching
   b. Vasant
   c. his foot resting on the ball
   d. toward the goal down the field from him
   e. looked intently

3. MODEL: Miss Toshiko Sasaki, **the East Asia Tin Works clerk, who was not related to Dr. Sasaki**, got up at three o'clock in the morning on the day the bomb fell.

> John Hersey, *Hiroshima*

   a. who was dedicated to on-time delivery
   b. George Smiley
   c. on the day the package was due
   d. the Federal Express driver
   e. drove up the congested street of the destination

4. MODEL: Sergeant Fales, **a big broad-faced man, who had fought in Panama and during the Gulf War**, felt anger with the pain.

> Mark Bowden, *Black Hawk Down*

   a. an agile long-legged gymnast
   b. and during the Olympics
   c. felt pride with her accomplishment
   d. Cheryl Lusky
   e. who had won in the preliminaries

5. MODEL: The market, **a large open square with wooden houses on two sides, some containing first-floor shops**, was crowded with peasant carts laden with grains, vegetables, wood, hides, and whatnot.

> Bernard Malamud, *The Fixer*

   a. the library
   b. one holding a calico cat
   c. was lined with bookshelves
   d. filled with classics, best-sellers, children's stories, magazines, and newspapers
   e. a warm, comfortable room with inviting chairs in cozy corners

PRACTICE 3: IMITATING

Identify the tools within the S-V split position in the models and sample imitations. Then write an imitation of each model, one sentence part at a time. Read one of your imitations to see if your classmates can guess which model you imitated.

Models:

1. Her husband, **the banker, who was a careful, shrewd man**, tried hard to make her happy.

Sherwood Anderson, Winesburg, Ohio

Sample: Her pet, **a sheepdog, who was a mammoth, wooly creature**, wanted only to keep her company.

2. Neville, **his face tear-streaked, clutching his wrist**, hobbled off with Madame Hooch, who had her arm around him.

J. K. Rowling, Harry Potter and the Sorcerer's Stone

Sample: Sebastian, **his eyes half open, returning to consciousness**, sat upright for the nurse, who had a wheelchair for him.

3. Jody, **who was helping Doubletree Mutt, the big serious dog, to dig out a gopher**, straightened up as the ranch hand sauntered out of the barn.

John Steinbeck, The Red Pony

Sample: Sally May, who was helping Lisa Marie, her earnest little sister, to read a new book, turned around as the nosy cat jumped onto the pages of the book.

4. This Northwestern decoration, **strong, animistic, stylized, polychromatic**, was several centuries ahead of its time.

Kenneth Brower, The Starship and the Canoe

Sample: The decorative pin, **shiny, colorful, polished, funky**, was clearly noticeable on Miranda's coat.

5. A woman, **young, tall, slender, draped in a neck-to-ankle madonna-blue robe, barefoot**, glided along the shore against the blazing sky, singing in a beautiful bell-like voice, a liquid sound floating on the air.

Christy Brown, Down All the Days

Sample: A phantom, **dark, alone, mysterious, clothed in a pearl-gray cape, booted**, climbed up the stairs toward the empty attic, moving in a careful cat-like motion, a feral energy coming from its presence.

PRACTICE 4: EXPANDING

The S-V split mix is omitted in the following sentences. Add an S-V split mix of different tools at the caret mark (^), blending your content and style with the rest of the sentence.

1. The twins, ^, followed them in a detached way.

   Katherine Anne Porter, *Ship of Fools*

2. Mrs. Botkin, ^, started to say something.

   Evan Connell Jr., "The Condor and the Guests"

3. The clerk, ^, tried to talk me into buying one big bottle.

   Robert Cormier, *Take Me Where the Good Times Are*

4. A bird somewhere, ^, called for its friends.

   Robert Lypsite, *The Contender*

5. A month later, at about four o'clock in the afternoon, a dusty old four-door green Packard car, ^, drove up to the Smith house.

   Fannie Flagg, *Standing in the Rainbow*

CREATIVE WRITING

Composing a paragraph—Pretend that you are one of the following authors who has written the first sentence of a long story. Choose one of the sentences listed as the first sentence in a paragraph that will begin that story. Create the rest of the paragraph.

Just as the writers' sentences use S-V split mixes, within your paragraph use S-V split mixes and other sentence-composing tools you've learned to make your paragraph memorable.

Reminder: Don't try to write a complete story. Write, revise, and finalize only the first paragraph of that story. (Maybe later you'll want to write the entire story!)

1. Meg, **moving the tip of her tongue over her teeth, which had only recently lost their braces**, looked at the boy affectionately and sadly. *(present participial phrase, adjective clause)*

   Madeleine L'Engle, *A Wind in the Door*

2. Some horses, **sleek** and **well-groomed**, trotted up across the grass and looked at them intently with very intelligent faces, and then off they galloped to the buildings. *(delayed adjective, past participial phrase)*

   J. R. R. Tolkien, *The Hobbit*

3. The depression, **which had been circling him ever since he left The Blue Door in Portland, circling the way wolves often circled campfires in the adventure stories he had read as a boy**, suddenly fell upon him. *(adjective clause, present participial phrase)*

   Stephen King, *Needful Things*

4. His voice, **soft and surprisingly high**, almost **like the voice of a woman**, wiped out any idea of cruelty. *(delayed adjectives, prepositional phrases)*

   Rosa Guy, *The Friends*

5. The great white bed, **huge as a prairie, composed of layer upon solid layer of mattress, blanket, and quilt**, almost filled the little shadowy room in which it stood. *(delayed adjective phrase, past participial phrase)*

   Joan Aiken, "Searching for Summer"

Tip for Better Revising: Always, when you revise something you've written, look for places to use a mixture of tools in the S-V split position plus other sentence-composing tools to add detail, interest, and style to your writing.

121

Closer Mix

DEFINITION

Two or more different tools at the end of a sentence. Mixing two or more different writer's tools within the closer position is common in professional writing. The tools can be any mix of the tools covered in this worktext.

Examples:

1. Court-appointed defenses were usually given to Maxwell Green, **Maycomb's latest addition to the bar, who needed the experience.** *(appositive phrase, adjective clause)*

   Harper Lee, *To Kill a Mockingbird*

2. It is likely that the space around the solar system is populated by huge numbers of comets, **small worlds a few miles in diameter, rich in water and the other chemicals essential to life.** *(appositive phrase, delayed adjective phrase)*

   Kenneth Brower, *The Starship and the Canoe*

3. The boys flew on and on, **toward the village, speechless with horror.** *(prepositional phrase, delayed adjective phrase)*

   Mark Twain, *The Adventures of Tom Sawyer*

4. There they all were now, **the cream of the school, the lights and leaders of the senior class, with their high I.Q.'s and expensive shoes, pasting each other with snowballs.** *(two appositive phrases, prepositional phrase, present participial phrase)*

   John Knowles, *A Separate Peace*

PRACTICE 1: MATCHING

Match the mixed tools with their sentences. Write out each sentence, inserting the tools at the caret (^) marks and underlining them. Name the tools.

Sentences:

1. Benny caught the boy by the shoulder ^.

   Hal Borland, *When the Legends Die*

Closer Mixes:

a. being tossed up in the air, his legs and arms like a doll's, limp and falling

2. Rivera was standing in the middle
   of the boxing ring, ^.

   Robert Lipsyte, *The Contender*

3. The iceberg towered, ^.

   Walter Lord, *A Night to Remember*

4. The Danes had destroyed their own
   naval fleet, ^.

   Lois Lowry, *Number the Stars*

5. The man invaded the bull's terrain
   too deeply, and he was on the bull's
   horns, ^.

   Maia Woiciechowska, *Shadow of a Bull*

b. blowing up the vessels one by one,
   as the Germans approached to take
   over the ships for their own use

c. before he could run to the bear,
   which was bawling and snapping
   at the chain

d. his feet flat on the lumpy canvas,
   planted like a tree

e. wet and glistening far above
   the forecastle deck of the *Titanic*

PRACTICE 2: UNSCRAMBLING TO IMITATE

In the model and the scrambled list, identify the closer mix and name the tools
within it. Next, unscramble and write out the sentence parts to imitate the model.
Finally, write your own imitation of the model and identify the closer mix.

1. MODEL: The ponies were scrambling up the beach, **on Assateague Beach, that
   long, sandy island that shelters the tidewater country of Virginia and
   Maryland.**

   Marguerite Henry, *Misty of Chincoteague*

   a. in Central Park
   b. that borders the gray skyscrapers of New York
   c. were laughing in the playground
   d. that green, inviting refuge
   e. the children

2. MODEL: The dinosaur had spit in his eye with acidy foam, and as he realized
   it, the pain overwhelmed him, and he dropped to his knees, **disoriented,
   wheezing.**

   Michael Crichton, *Jurassic Park*

a. dazed

b. the deer had leaped over the fence in an abrupt shift

c. sudden confusion overtook it

d. but when it hit the ground

e. staggering

f. and it turned in all directions

3. MODEL: Roger was short and bald, **his baldness offset by rich bushy black-and-grey eyebrows and a short beard, which lent him a twinkling impishness.**

Frank McCourt, *Teacher Man*

a. about literary symbolism and stylistic devices

b. the project

c. the length caused by elaborate, detailed explanations

d. was complex and long

e. which made it a challenging long-range assignment

4. MODEL: Now I spotted it, **the address in the 200 block, an old, pseudo-modernized office building, tired, outdated, refusing to admit it** but **unable to hide it.**

Jack Finney, "Of Missing Persons"

a. wanting to pick a fight

b. a mean, oversized ugly troublemaker

c. the bully of the gym class

d. but trying to deny it

e. then the teacher reprimanded the student

f. agitated, frustrated

5. MODEL: For a moment, Cecilia stood alone in the center of the room, **fluttering the fingers of her right hand, staring at them each in turn, unable to believe her association with such people, unable to tell them what she knew.**

Ian McEwan, *Atonement*

a. in the evening

b. studying the pages of his favorite book

c. able to accompany them wherever they went

d. glancing at them one at a time

e. Harry retired quietly to the storage room in the attic

f. able to imagine himself with every character

PRACTICE 3: IMITATING

Identify the tools within the closer position in the models and sample imitations. Then write an imitation of each model, one sentence part at a time. Read one of your imitations to see if your classmates can guess which model you imitated.

Models:

1. It was good to sit there in Charley's kitchen, **my coat and tie flung over a chair, surrounded by soul food and love.**

    Eugenia Collier, "Sweet Potato Pie"

    Sample: It was peaceful to bask there on the open beach, **my body and soul spread out on a towel, clothed by warm sun and sand.**

2. They tramped off, **anxious** and **downhearted, under the eyes of the crowd.**

    J. R. R. Tolkien, *The Lord of the Rings*

    Sample: The faculty sat down, **silent** and **interested, for the report of the principal.**

3. The locusts were flopping against her, and she brushed them off, **heavy red-brown creatures, looking at her with their beady old-men's eyes while they clung with hard, serrated legs.**

    Doris Lessing, "A Mild Attack of Locusts"

    Sample: The ideas were filling inside him, and he considered each one, **creative, never-ending high, wide, rich ideas, pouring from his cavernous mind as if they burst from a high, wide dam.**

4. Hattie sat down at her old Spanish table, **watching them in the cloudy warmth of the day, clasping her hands, sad** and **chuckling.**

    Saul Bellow, "Leaving the Yellow House"

    Sample: Henry watched over the scared, refugee children, **holding them with the gentle touch of his hands, singing a soft lullaby, comforting** and **lovely.**

5. At midmorning, the sailors had caught an enormous shark, **which died on deck, thrashing wickedly in its death throes, while no one dared to go near enough to club it.**

    Isabel Allende, *Daughter of Fortune*

Sample: At dusk, the campers had seen several deer, **which grazed on the grass, moving gently across the lower pasture, while no other animals tried to move close enough to frighten them.**

PRACTICE 4: EXPANDING

The closer mix is omitted in the following sentences. Add a closer mix of different tools at the caret mark (^), blending your content and style with the rest of the sentence.

1. She was in the doorway, ^.

    John Christopher, *The Guardians*

2. There were two people there, ^.

    Michael Crichton, *Prey*

3. He was twenty at the time, ^.

    Anne Tyler, *The Amateur Marriage*

4. He spent three days propped up in bed, ^.

    Fannie Flagg, *Standing in the Rainbow*

5. This was a moment she normally savored, ^.

    P. D. James, *A Certain Justice*

CREATIVE WRITING

Composing a paragraph—Pretend that you are one of the following authors who has written the first sentence of a long story. Choose one of the sentences listed as the first sentence in a paragraph that will begin that story. Create the rest of the paragraph.

Just as the writers' sentences use closer mixes, within your paragraph use closer mixes and other sentence-composing tools you've learned to make your paragraph memorable.

Reminder: Don't try to write a complete story. Write, revise, and finalize only the first paragraph of that story. (Maybe later you'll want to write the entire story!)

1. An hour later she drove over in her father's pickup, **smiling, her hair down on her shoulders, mouth radiant with lipstick.** *(present participle, two absolute phrases)*

    Stephen King, *Hearts in Atlantis*

2. Papa sat on a bench in the barn, **his broken leg stretched awkwardly before him, mending one of Jack's harnesses.** *(absolute phrase, present participial phrase)*

   Mildred D. Taylor, *Roll of Thunder, Hear My Cry*

3. It was a pitiful sight, **the three of us in our overcoats and boots, standing among the dead stalks of winter.** *(appositive phrase, present participial phrase)*

   Cynthia Rylant, *Missing May*

4. The Palace Hotel at Fort Romper was painted a light blue, **a shade that is on the legs of a kind of heron, causing the bird to declare its position against any background.** *(appositive phrase, present participial phrase)*

   Stephen Crane, "The Blue Hotel"

5. He trembled alone there in the middle of the park for hours, **wondering what would happen if he had an attack of appendicitis, unnerved by the thoughts of a fainting spell, horrified by the realization that he might have to move his bowels, until at last we came.** *(present participial phrase, two past participial phrases, adverb clause)*

   John Knowles, *A Separate Peace*

Tip for Better Revising: Always, when you revise something you've written, look for places to use a mixture of tools in the closing position plus other sentence-composing tools to add detail, interest, and style to your writing.

Other Mix

DEFINITION

Tools within different positions within the same sentence: opener, S-V split, closer. Tools separated from each other are common in professional writing. The tools can be any mix of the tools covered in this worktext.

Examples:

These sentences illustrate the use of different sentence-composing tools within two or three of the positions: opener, S-V split, closer. The result is an upgraded sentence, like a highly accessorized instead of stripped car.

To see the difference, read each sentence below twice: first with the tools, then without. Like accessories on a new car, sentence-composing tools boost style and value.

Opener and S-V Split:

1. **As they looked up**, two young policemen, **accompanied by a man in a uniform like a streetcar conductor's**, swept around the corner and dashed straight into the restaurant. *(adverb clause, past participial phrase)*

   Henry Sydnor Harrison, "Miss Hinch"

Opener and Closer:

2. **Later, when it was dark**, they returned to the car lot, **exhausted and laughing, drinking beer from brown paper bags.** *(opening adverb, adverb clause, past participle, present participle, present participial phrase)*

   Mitch Albom, *The Five People You Meet in Heaven*

S-V Split and Closer:

3. The Scuppernong grapevine, **a gift from his mother's kin in Carolina**, was in bloom for the first time, **fine** and **lace-like**. *(appositive phrase, delayed adjectives)*

   Marjorie Kinnan Rawlings, *The Yearling*

Opener, S-V Split, and Closer:

4. **Suddenly**, the chandelier, **an immense mass of crystal**, was slipping down from the ceiling, **coming toward the terrified audience, at the call of the Phantom's fiendish voice.** *(opening adverb, appositive phrase, present participial phase, prepositional phrase)*

   Gaston Leroux, *The Phantom of the Opera*

PRACTICE 1: MATCHING

Match the mixed tools with their sentences. Write out each sentence, inserting the tools at the caret (^) marks and underlining them. Name the tools and positions.

Sentences:

1. ^, there was a freak plant, ^.

   Carson McCullers, *The Heart Is a Lonely Hunter*

2. Mrs. Hatching, ^, stood looking at them proudly, ^.

   Joan Aiken, "Searching for Summer"

3. ^, she rested after the climb, ^.

   Charles Frazier, *Cold Mountain*

4. ^, she would sit at her desk, ^.

   Truman Capote, *The Grass Harp*

5. ^, she had noticed very soon one little girl, ^.

   Frances Hodgson Burnett, *A Little Princess*

Tools:

a. after supper, wearing a green eye-shade / totaling figures and turning the pages of her ledgers until the street-lamps had gone out

b. when she reached to the crest of the ridge / sitting on a rock outcrop that commanded a prospect back into the river valley

c. among the flowers / a zinnia with six bronze petals and two red

d. on that first morning, when Sara sat at Miss Munchkin's side, aware that the whole schoolroom was devoting itself to observing her / about her own age, who looked at her very hard with a pair of light, rather dull, blue eyes.

e. silent for the moment / her bright eyes slowly moving from face to face

PRACTICE 2: UNSCRAMBLING TO IMITATE

In the model and the scrambled list, identify the mixed tools within various positions. Next, unscramble and write out the sentence parts to imitate the model. Finally, write your own imitation of the model and identify the mixed tools within different positions.

1. MODEL: **In an explosion of dirt and pebbles**, the pig burst from under the fence, **heaving Taran into the air.**

   Lloyd Alexander, *The Book of Three*

   a. looked out from behind a bush
   b. Jeremy
   c. spying a rattlesnake on a rock
   d. of gravel and dirt
   e. near a path

2. MODEL: Gabriel, **wrapped in his inadequate blanket**, was hunched, **shivering**, and **silent in his little seat**.

   Lois Lowry, *The Giver*

   a. silenced by his demanding coach
   b. Rafael
   c. and resentful of the coach's condescending tone
   d. was humiliated
   e. crying

3. MODEL: **With the first paling of the sky**, a roped file of men, **bent almost double beneath heavy loads**, began slowly to climb the ice slope just beneath the jagged line of the great last ridge.

   James Ramsey Ullman, *Banner in the Sky*

   a. raced eagerly to enter their beloved cars
   b. a cheerful collection of students
   c. after the final bell of the day
   d. right outside the rear entrance to the academic high school
   e. released pretty much from class demands

4. MODEL: **After a little while**, Mr. Gatz opened the door and came out, **his mouth ajar, his face flushed slightly, his eyes leaking isolated and unpunctual tears.**

   F. Scott Fitzgerald, *The Great Gatsby*

   a. the skaters came off the ice and sat down
   b. their breath quieting
   c. their minds thinking energizing and hopeful thoughts
   d. their heartbeats calming gradually
   e. during the short break

5. MODEL: That one letter, **scrawled on the floor with a broken bit of yellow chalk gripped between my toes**, was my road to a new world, **my key to mental freedom**.

Christy Brown, Down All the Days

   a. the destruction of growing confidence
   b. uttered in the anger of a thoughtless taunt
   c. was the ruination of a blossoming spirit
   d. that single word
   e. about small players shunned by the team

PRACTICE 3: IMITATING

Identify the tools and their positions in the models and sample imitations. Then write an imitation of each model, one sentence part at a time. Read one of your imitations to see if your classmates can guess which model you imitated.

Models:

1. **His face lit by flames**, across the open hearth sat my father, **leaning forward, hands outspread on his knees, his shoulders tense**.

Christy Brown, Down All the Days

Sample: Her tears held in check, in the kitchen stood my sister, looking pale, eyes wide in her face, her hair disheveled.

2. Arawn, **the dread Lord of Annuvin**, comes from the Mabinogion, **the classic collection of Welsh legends, although in Prydain he is considerably more villainous**.

Lloyd Alexander, The Book of Three

Sample: Antonio, the toughest member of the class, came from the suburbs, a notorious area outside New York City, although in our club he is considerably more gentlemanly.

3. **Warm** and **dusty** and **over-wearied**, he came to our door and eased his heavy pack and asked for refreshment, and Devola brought him a pail of water from our spring, **pure** and **so cold it made him clench his teeth**.

Bill and Vera Cleaver, Where the Lilies Bloom

Sample: Small and sweet but overtired, she sat in her crib and scratched her little head and looked for company, and Myra gave her a bear of velvet from the playpen, soft and so cuddly it made her touch its tummy.

4. **After a word with the lieutenant**, he went a few paces higher and sat there, **a dominant figure, his sweat-marked horse swishing its tail, while he looked down on his men**.

D. H. Lawrence, "The Prussian Officer"

Sample: After that comment from the group, he withdrew a little bit farther and stood there, a shy observer, his clear, thick glasses magnifying his eyes, as he blinked nervously at the group.

5. **Through the door**, I could hear Donna Kabrisky, **the secretary I shared with Bob Trope, talking on the phone**.

John Burnham Schwartz, *Reservation Road*

Sample: Out the window, we could see Quentin Ogilby, the neighbor we distrusted without hesitation, yelling at the mailman.

PRACTICE 4: EXPANDING

The tools are omitted in the following sentences. Add a variety of tools at each caret mark (^), blending your content and style with the rest of the sentence.

1. The only other person in the room, ^, came over to Jelly, ^.
Robert Lipsyte, *The Contender*

2. ^, we hastened along the invisible road, ^.
Mildred D. Taylor, *Roll of Thunder, Hear My Cry*

3. Beneath the dragon, ^, lay countless piles of precious things, ^.
J. R. R. Tolkien, *The Hobbit*

4. ^, she wandered about the pillared rooms, ^.
Ray Bradbury, *The Martian Chronicles*

5. ^, two of the creatures, ^, stood looking at him, ^.
Alexander Key, *The Forgotten Door*

CREATIVE WRITING

Composing a paragraph—Pretend that you are one of the following authors who has written the first sentence of a long story. Choose one of the sentences listed as the first sentence in a paragraph that will begin that story. Create the rest of the paragraph.

Just as the writers' sentences use mixed tools within various positions, within your paragraph use mixed tools within various positions and other sentence-composing tools you've learned to make your paragraph memorable.

Reminder: Don't try to write a complete story. Write, revise, and finalize only the first paragraph of that story. (Maybe later you'll want to write the entire story!)

1. **At the foot of one of the trees**, the boy's father sat, **the lantern still burning by his side**. *(opener: prepositional phrases; closer: absolute phrase)*

   William H. Armstrong, *Sounder*

2. A wild-eyed horse, **its bridle torn and dangling**, trotted frantically through the mounds of men, **tossing its head, whinnying in panic**. *(S-V split: absolute phrase; closers: present participial phrases)*

   Lois Lowry, *The Giver*

3. There, **placed on one of the hooks above the woodbox**, was my high-school jacket, **the one with the big white GF entwined on the breast**. *(opener: past participial phrase; closer: appositive phrase)*

   Stephen King, *Hearts in Atlantis*

4. **Suddenly, with shocking speed**, the fog cleared, **the particles coalescing into two fully formed columns that now stood directly before us, rising and falling in dark ripples**. *(openers: opening adverb, prepositional phrase; closers: absolute phrase, present participial phrases)*

   Michael Crichton, *Prey*

5. The scrub, **that big wild stretch of dry and sandy land where scrub oaks, scrub pines, and palmettos grew**, was an unexplored wilderness, **always beckoning to the children**. *(S-V split: appositive phrase; closer: present participial phrase)*

   Lois Lenski, *Strawberry Girl*

Tip for Better Revising: Always, when you revise something you've written, look for places to use a mixture of tools in different positions plus other sentence-composing tools to add detail, interest, and style to your writing.

To make sense, sentences need punctuation marks. The following sentence, because punctuation has been removed, is hard to understand.

Without punctuation: Three figures leaned against the slanting rain Alamo Laska Nick Christopher and the boy who had run away from home.

This sentence is puzzling. Isn't an Alamo a historical building? But what could a "slanting rain Alamo" be? If Alamo isn't a building, is it a name or part of a name? But there are four names and only "three figures" indicated.

Which words go together? We could guess, but reading shouldn't be a guessing game.

If correct punctuation were included in the sentence, we'd understand it easily. Here's the sentence correctly punctuated, and no longer puzzling.

With punctuation: Three figures leaned against the slanting rain: Alamo Laska, Nick Christopher, and the boy who had run away from home.

Edmund Ware, "An Underground Episode"

Without the colon to introduce the list, the sentence wouldn't be so easily understood. Effective writers use a wide range of punctuation marks (not only commas). Each of the following sentences illustrates how they frequently use certain "professional" punctuation marks: semicolons, colons, dashes.

Semicolon:

1. There was talk that her father and mother were taking her back to Earth next year; it seemed vital to her that they do so, though it would mean the loss of thousands of dollars to her family.

   Ray Bradbury, "All Summer in a Day"

2. People didn't go to ocean piers much anymore; they went to theme parks where you paid lots for a ticket and had your photo taken with a giant furry character.

   Mitch Albom, *The Five People You Meet in Heaven*

3. Sweat popped out on the boy's face; he began to struggle.

   Langston Hughes, "Thank You, M'am"

Colon:

1. It is more than just wind: it is a solid wall of snow moving at gale force, pounding like surf.

    Richard E. Byrd, *Alone*

2. In the beginning, in the evenings, his family went for drives, exploring their new environs bit by bit: the neglected dirt lanes, the shaded back roads, the farms where one could pick pumpkins in autumn and buy berries sold in green cardboard boxes in July.

    Jhumpa Lahiri, *The Namesake*

3. When he reached the door, he realized what had attracted him: the smell of food.

    Franz Kafka, *The Metamorphosis*

Dash:

1. Because he was still able to move his hands—Morrie always spoke with both hands waving—he showed great passion when explaining how you face the end of life.

    Mitch Albom, *Tuesdays with Morrie*

2. His room looked smaller now—not so much a place to come to as a place to leave.

    Stephen King, *Hearts in Atlantis*

3. A man with murder in his heart will murder, or be murdered—it comes to the same thing—and so I knew I had to leave.

    James Baldwin, "Every Good-bye Ain't Gone"

*****

Knowing how to use semicolons, colons, and dashes opens up new ways to build better sentences. The fact that most authors choose to use those three marks suggests that they contribute to good sentences.

Punctuating Like a Pro: Semicolon

DEFINITION

A punctuation mark to join two sentences about the same thing. A semicolon tells the reader that the ideas in two sentences are closely related. Even though two sentences are linked by a semicolon, only the first sentence is capitalized.

Examples:

1. People didn't go to ocean piers much anymore; they went to theme parks where you paid lots for a ticket and had your photo taken with a giant furry character.

Mitch Albom, The Five People You Meet in Heaven

2. Sweat popped out on the boy's face; he began to struggle.

Langston Hughes, "Thank You, M'am"

Each could have been written as two separate sentences:

1. People didn't go to ocean piers much anymore. They went to theme parks where you paid lots for a ticket and had your photo taken with a giant furry character.

2. Sweat popped out on the boy's face. He began to struggle.

Instead, the authors chose to express the content as one sentence with a semicolon because of the close content link between them.

PRACTICE 1: MATCHING

Match the sentence with a semicolon in the left column to the related sentence in the right column. Write out the result.

Sentences with Semicolons: **Related Sentences:**

1. A beam of light fell across the grass,   a. only the present remains
   hit the bottom of the tree, and
   illuminated its branches; ^

   J. K. Rowling, *Harry Potter and the Prisoner of Azkaban*

2. Sometimes the mountain was brilliant above us, as it had been when we first saw it; ^.

   James Ramsey Ullman, *Banner in the Sky*

   b. in some places, where the seaweed wasn't too thick, you could see the bottom

3. That night Tao Chi'en realized that he could not care for Eliza alone; ^.

   Isabel Allende, *Daughter of Fortune*

   c. there, crouching among the budding leaves, was Crookshanks

4. The past and the future are cut off; ^.

   Anne Morrow Lindbergh, *Gift from the Sea*

   d. he needed help

5. The water was wonderfully calm; ^.

   Monica Charles, *To Live with a Legend*

   e. sometimes it was partially or wholly obscured by tiers of clouds

PRACTICE 2: UNSCRAMBLING TO IMITATE

Explain why the semicolon in the model is correct. Next, unscramble and write out the sentence parts to imitate the model. Begin with the sentence part set in **boldface**. Finally, write your own imitation of the model.

1. MODEL: A few stray white bread crumbs lay on the cleanly washed floor by the table; putting the lamp upon a low stool, he began to pick up the crumbs.

   Sherwood Anderson, *Winesburg, Ohio*

   a. **Some frisky little kids**
   b. leaping them a step at a time
   c. ran around the newly built hall of the elementary school
   d. they started to run up the stairs

2. MODEL: A tall, shambling dark young fellow had gone ashore and was now re-turning; he lounged along in the wake of the Spanish girls, regarding them with what could only be described as a leer.

   Katherine Anne Porter, *Ship of Fools*

   a. **The penniless, new freshman college student**
   b. with what might be described as a panic
   c. had written home and was now waiting
   d. he walked quickly toward the mailboxes of the first-year dormitory
   e. approaching them

3. MODEL: He has always wished they were on the eastern side of the building, preferring to look out on frozen cliffs of water in winter, rather than dirty streets, dirtier cars; it is not a pleasant corner in the midst of the gray Chicago winter.

Judith Guest, *Ordinary People*

   a. **She had never hoped she would be in the semifinals of the high diving competition**
   b. with her difficult academic program
   c. wanting to check out of the entire world of sports in high school
   d. in the middle of her struggles
   e. rather than constant practice, constant stress
   f. competition was not a great idea

4. MODEL: Gollum wanted the ring because it was a ring of power, and if you slipped that ring on your finger, you were invisible; only in the full sunlight could you be seen, and then only by your shadow, and that would be shaky and faint.

J. R. R. Tolkien, *The Hobbit*

   a. **Alfred visited the museum**
   b. and then only for a year
   c. because it was a source of employment
   d. and if he got that job as an apprentice
   e. he would be content
   f. but that would be encouraging and helpful
   g. only after an apprenticeship could he be hired

5. MODEL: For a moment Augustus thought of throwing himself in the way of the horses to stop them, but before the carriage reached him, something gave way; one of the horses detached itself from the carriage and came galloping past him.

Isak Dinesen, "The Roads Round Pisa"

   a. **After a while Samantha thought**
   b. things changed
   c. but after she reached the station
   d. one of her conspirators called her from his cell phone
   e. of turning herself in to the police
   f. and started yelling at her
   g. to end it

PRACTICE 3: EXPANDING

The following sentences are either to the left or to the right of a semicolon. Add content that would make sense with the rest of the sentence, making sure that what you add is a sentence, not a sentence part.

1. **An Otter Stalking a Trout**
   He came to the corner of the rock and paused, sank until his belly softly scraped the sand, and became one with the bottom's shadows; *(sentence)*.

   Robert Murphy, "You've Got to Learn"

2. **The Contents of the Back of the Pickup Truck**
   His pickup truck was parked outside the gate; *(sentence)*.

   Walter Lord, *A Night to Remember*

3. **A Man Preparing to Cook Dinner**
   (sentence); he set a kettle of water on the stove and dropped a can of beans into the water.

   John Steinbeck, "The Snake"

4. **A Trapped Elephant Trying to Get Free**
   Sometimes the elephant would get his tusks stuck between the bars of the cage and snort irritably as he tried to get free; *(sentence)*.

   Michael Crichton, *Jurassic Park*

5. **A Child Leaving Home for the First Day of Kindergarten**
   (sentence); I watched him go off the first morning with the older girl next door, seeing clearly that an era of my life was ended, my sweet-voiced nursery-school tot replaced by a long-trousered swaggering character who forgot to stop at the corner and wave good-bye to me.

   Shirley Jackson, "Charles"

Punctuating Like a Pro: Colon

DEFINITION

A punctuation mark used to signal a list or an explanation. An introductory sentence precedes the colon telling the reader what to expect: a list or an explanation.

Examples:

1. It is more than just wind: it is a solid wall of snow moving at gale force, pounding like surf.

   Richard E. Byrd, *Alone*

2. In the beginning, in the evenings, his family went for drives, exploring their new environs bit by bit: the neglected dirt lanes, the shaded back roads, the farms where one could pick pumpkins in autumn and buy berries sold in green cardboard boxes in July.

   Jhumpa Lahiri, *The Namesake*

3. When he reached the door, he realized what had attracted him: the smell of food.

   Franz Kafka, *The Metamorphosis*

Sentences 1 and 3 have a colon signaling an explanation: in sentence 1, the reason it was stronger than a wind, and in 3, the reason he was attracted. Sentence 2 contains a colon signaling a list of attractions the family saw during evening drives in their community.

There is one rule for writing sentences with colons: everything to the left of the colon must be a complete sentence. Read the three sentences again. Notice that everything to the left of each colon is a complete sentence. To the right of the colon can be either a complete sentence (sentence 1) or not (2 and 3). Either is okay, but to the left of the colon must always be a complete sentence.

A colon is the equals sign of punctuation: everything to the left of a colon must equal everything to the right of the colon.

Examples:

1. **List:** There were toys on the floor: a rolling yellow ball, a doll, a plastic rattle.

   Michael Crichton, *Jurassic Park*

   In this list, the toys mentioned to the left of the colon equal the ones listed to the right of the colon. *Toys = ball, doll, rattle.*

2. **Explanation:** That spring was a good one: the days grew longer and gave us more playing time.

   Harper Lee, *To Kill a Mockingbird*

   In this explanation, the good spring mentioned to the left of the colon equals the longer days with more playing time mentioned to the right of the colon. *Good spring = longer days with more playing time.*

   When you use a colon for a list or an explanation, be sure that what's on the left equals what's on the right.

PRACTICE 1: MATCHING

Match the sentence with a colon in the left column to the list or explanation in the right column. Write out the result.

Sentences with Colons:

1. They learned the names of the different architectural styles: ^.

   Jhumpa Lahiri, *The Namesake*

2. Then she heard it: ^.

   Jessamyn West, "The Child's Day"

3. The woman brought out three outfits: ^.

   Gary Soto, "Barbie"

4. The writing would be awful: ^.

   Christy Brown, *My Left Foot*

5. Word carpentry is like any other kind of carpentry: ^.

   Anatole France (quotation about writing)

List or Explanation:

a. the sound she had been born to hear, the footstep her ears had been made to echo

b. a summer dress, a pants suit, and a lacy gown the color of mother-of-pearl

c. cape, saltbox, raised ranch, garrison

d. huge, scrawling words sloping horizontally down the page with no dots, dashes or commas between them and, of course, no such thing as a question or exclamation mark anywhere

e. you must join your sentences smoothly

PRACTICE 2: UNSCRAMBLING TO IMITATE

Explain why the colon in the model is correct. Next, unscramble and write out the sentence parts to imitate the model. Begin with the sentence part in **boldface**. Finally, write your own imitation of the model.

1. MODEL: Whether he was being brilliant or dull, he had one sole topic of conversation: himself.

   Deems Taylor, "The Monster"

  a. **Whenever she was either bored or irritated**
  b. withdrawal
  c. she had only one way of responding

2. MODEL: This was what I feared when I lifted the dark-green shade: I feared a face outside the window, dead eyes looking in at me as I pulled out of sleep.

   Mary Gordon, *Final Payments*

  a. **This was what I loved**
  b. as I sank slowly into serenity
  c. when I closed my heavy-lidded eyes
  d. beautiful waves tumbling in at my feet
  e. I loved a dream about the beach

3. MODEL: He has caught her off-guard, but she is still more poised than he, and this close he can see her face: small, delicate features, the casual elegance of a painter or a dancer, a beautiful pointed nose.

   Judith Guest, *Ordinary People*

  a. **She had seen him suddenly**
  b. frantic, darting excitement
  c. and she was not prepared for it
  d. an awful uncontrollable crush
  e. the growing anticipation of a child or an actor
  f. so this time she would anticipate her emotions

4. MODEL: His real history is much longer and much more extraordinary than could be indicated by these flares of war: it is history that runs back three centuries into primitive America, a strange and unfathomable history that is touched by something dark and supernatural.

   Thomas Wolfe, "The Men of Old Catawba"

  a. **Her awful secret is more horrible and a lot more painful**
  b. it is a secret that goes
  c. a dark and desperate secret
  d. into other circumstances from her past
  e. than could be revealed in these tapes of interviews
  f. that is rooted in something terrifying and heart-breaking

5. MODEL: He sketched what he saw through the iron window bars: the crooked skyline, the courtyards, the cobblestone square where he watched maids filling

brass urns at the tube well, people passing under the soiled canopies of rick-shaws, hurrying home with parcels in the rain.

Jhumpa Lahiri, *The Namesake*

a. **She reviewed what she had from her worn, old purse**
b. the beat-up wallet
c. receipts crumpled into little handfuls of paper
d. the ticket stub, the comb
e. where she kept pictures showing family members at various celebrations
f. reminding her of purchases from the past

PRACTICE 3: EXPANDING

The following contain part of a sentence with a colon. Add content described in the parentheses.

1. **An Old Man Trying to Escape**
   He could never escape them, no matter how much or how far he ran: *(explanation)*.

   William Faulkner, "Wash"

2. **List of Five Achievements**
   So much had been achieved: senior rank, a prestigious job with a boss she liked and admired, *(list of three more achievements)*.

   P. D. James, *A Certain Justice*

3. **A Man Awakening to Bad News**
   I awoke to a jolting piece of news: *(explanation)*.

   Mitch Albom, *Tuesdays with Morrie*

4. **List of Eight Topics in Her Letter or Email**
   She wrote of many things: her new curtains, the hot summer, the coat she had had remodeled, *(list of five more topics)*.

   Nancy and Benedict Freedman, *Mrs. Mike*

5. **A Precious Object**
   Not far away was Gollum's island, of which Bilbo knew nothing, and there in his hiding-place he kept a few wretched oddments, and one very beautiful thing, very beautiful, very wonderful: *(explanation)*.

   J. R. R. Tolkien, *The Hobbit*

Punctuating Like a Pro: Dash

DEFINITION

A punctuation mark to interrupt a sentence in the middle or at the end. If the interruption is in the middle of a sentence, two dashes are used, one before the interruption, one after. If the interruption is at the end of a sentence, one dash is used. A dash tells the reader to expect a kind of "P.S." or "by the way" or other kind of afterthought. *Typing Tip:* A dash is made by hitting the hyphen key twice, not once.

Examples:

1. Because he was still able to move his hands—Morrie always spoke with both hands waving—he showed great passion when explaining how you face the end of life.

   Mitch Albom, *Tuesdays with Morrie*

2. His room looked smaller now—not so much a place to come to as a place to leave.

   Stephen King, *Hearts in Atlantis*

3. A man with murder in his heart will murder, or be murdered—it comes to the same thing—and so I knew I had to leave.

   James Baldwin, "Every Good-bye Ain't Gone"

Dashes indicate abruptness: a shift in thought, a change of topics, a conversational "P.S." within the same sentence. The interruption itself can be either a sentence or a sentence part. In sentences 1 and 3, it is a sentence; in sentence 2, a sentence part.

PRACTICE 1: MATCHING

Match the interruption from the right column to the sentence in the left column. Write out the result.

Sentences with Dashes:

1. On her mind was the supper she wanted to fix for Paul D ^ to launch her newer, stronger life with a tender man.

   Toni Morrison, *Beloved*

Interruptions:

a. they saved it all

2. Next day Dad came home with more news—^.

    Phyllis Reynolds Naylor, *Shiloh*

    b. good news to him, bad news to me

3. The house was crammed with ancient and dusty junk—^—from the attic to the cellar.

    Annie Proulx, "Dump Junk"

    c. a poacher, stealing off with his coat bulging with pheasants and partridges to drop them stealthily into a three-legged pot in his smoky little cottage

4. Now she saw him as he was—^.

    Virginia Woolf, "Lappin and Lapinova"

    d. something difficult to do, something she would do just so

5. Although we imagine we live in different nations—^—in fact we inhabit the same state, the State of Fear.

    Michael Crichton, *State of Fear*

    e. France, Germany, Japan, the U. S.

PRACTICE 2: UNSCRAMBLING TO IMITATE

Explain why the dashes in the models are correct. Next, unscramble and write out the sentence parts to imitate the model. Begin with the sentence part set in **bold-face**. Finally, write your own imitation of the model.

1. MODEL: There were three others with us—Finny in those days almost always moved in groups the size of a hockey team—and they stood with me looking with masked apprehension from him to the tree.

    John Knowles, *A Separate Peace*

    a. **There were older girls with us**
    b. about our uniforms from our school
    c. Clare in middle school frequently played
    d. and they remained with us
    e. kidding with slight sarcasm
    f. with girls the same age as the rest of us

2 MODEL: She walked back towards him, arms outstretched as though on a tight-rope, pretending to wobble—it's the sort of thing a character in an American soap might do when she wants important good news wrung from her.

    Ian McEwan, *Saturday*

a. **He leaned in toward Jackson**
b. when he intended quick easy compliance
c. eyes riveted as though on a criminal
d. it's the kind of behavior a policeman in a criminal investigation would try
e. forced from the suspect
f. starting to intimidate

3. MODEL: Over the table, where a collection of cloth samples was scattered—Samsa was a frequent traveler—hung the picture that he had recently cut from an illustrated paper and had put in a pretty gilded frame.

Franz Kafka, The Metamorphosis

a. **In the kitchen**
b. that she had just brought from the living room
c. Jenny had a huge sweet tooth
d. and had placed on the already cluttered counter
e. sat the plate
f. where a collection of cookie jars was arranged

4. MODEL: It had taken Crocker and his team—young men, all in good condition, with some money and supplies plus horses and wagons—almost half a year to cross the plains and mountains.

Stephen E. Ambrose, Nothing Like It in the World

a. **She had given Melinda and her family**
b. with no food and clothing or medicine and supplies
c. hurricane refugees
d. to buy some fast food and used clothing
e. all in desperate need
f. almost half her bonus

5. MODEL: Barry's family—his brother and sister-in-law, plus a couple of cousins—kept admiring this and that, asking if the dining-room fireplace actually functioned and if the people in the portraits were actual ancestors.

Anne Tyler, Back When We Were Grownups

a. **Brookie's pets**
b. started chewing rugs and furniture
c. plus a couple of hamsters
d. and when the contents of their dinners had been very bland
e. gnawing when the family members weren't looking
f. a cat and dog

PRACTICE 3: EXPANDING

Add content that would make sense with the rest of the sentence, making sure that what you add interrupts the sentence.

1. **Grandmother, the Only Witness**

   He then called the medical officer, who confirmed that a nine-day-old infant, sleeping in its crib, had been bitten on the foot by an animal the grandmother—*(interruption)*—claimed was a lizard.

   Michael Crichton, *Jurassic Park*

2. **New England**

   It had been a shock to Mitchell, after several years in Wyoming, to see New England again—*(interruption)*.

   Annie Proulx, "Man Crawling Out of Trees"

3. **Daisy's Way of Entering a Place**

   He heard the front-door lock turning, and by the sound of the door opening and closing—*(interruption)*—he knew it was Daisy.

   Ian McEwan, *Saturday*

4. **An Ordinary Building**

   It was such an ordinary, prosaic place here—*(interruption)*.

   E. Everett Evans, "The Shed"

5. **The Exact Moment of the Incident**

   The third day—*(interruption)*—Charles bounced a seesaw onto the head of a little girl and made her bleed, and the teacher made him stay inside all during recess.

   Shirley Jackson, "Charles"

Punctuating Like a Pro: Review

Semicolon—Joins two sentences about the same thing. A semicolon tells the reader that the ideas in two sentences are closely related.

Colon—Signals a list or an explanation. An introductory sentence precedes the colon to preview for readers what to expect: either a list or an explanation.

Dash—Interrupts a sentence in the middle or at the end. If the interruption is in the middle of a sentence, two dashes are used, one before the interruption, one after it. If the interruption is at the end, one dash is used.

DIRECTIONS: Punctuate each sentence by adding a semicolon, colon, or dash.

1. The mountains were miles away from the house of the family, and sometimes they were altogether hidden by weather cloud, rain, or wind alive with dust.
    Paul Horgan, "To the Mountains"

2. He made another vow that he would keep to the end of his life he would never do any work that exploited someone else, and he would never allow himself to make money off the sweat of others.
    Mitch Albom, *Tuesdays with Morrie*

3. Since it was late afternoon that time is prime telemarketing time we braced for one more unwelcome sales pitch.
    P. M. Forni, *Choosing Civility*

4. We had a dispute about whether the rider had to be on his horse at the finish, and it happened so often that the horse came in alone that we made a rule a horse, with or without his rider, won or lost the race.
    Lincoln Steffens, *A Boy on Horseback*

5. Suppose a ridiculous supposition, I know, but just suppose we fell in love and ended up together.
    Tobias Wolff, *Old School*

6. There is a scar on my husband's head his hair hides it.
    John Christopher, *The Guardians*

7. She is surprised to hear certain things about his life that all his parents' friends are Bengali, that they had had an arranged marriage, that his mother cooks Indian food every day, that she wears saris and a bindi.

Jhumpa Lahiri, *The Namesake*

8. The bombardment was finished once the jets had sighted their target and alerted their bombardier as quick as the whisper of a scythe, the war was finished.

Ray Bradbury, *Fahrenheit 451*

9. In the hospital, she learned a simple, obvious thing that she had always known, and everyone knew that a person is, among all else, a material thing, easily torn, not easily mended.

Ian McEwan, *Atonement*

10. Sarah Jones was profoundly distressed by the fact that George Morton's body had been recovered in some part of her mind, she had been hoping against hope that he would turn up alive.

Michael Crichton, *State of Fear*

In this final section of *Grammar for High School: A Sentence-Composing Approach*, you'll study the sentences of William Golding, author of *Lord of the Flies*, by identifying in his sentences the fourteen tools and special punctuation you've learned in this worktext, then imitating his sentences, and finally writing a new episode for *Lord of the Flies* with your own sentences built like the ones in Golding's novel.

In the following practices, notice how William Golding builds his sentences, using within his sentences the fourteen tools you've learned. If you need to review the tools, study the pages listed.

Words	Review These Pages
opening adjective = OADJ	14–17
delayed adjective = DADJ	18–21
opening adverb = OADV	22–25
delayed adverb = DADV	26–29

Phrases	Review These Pages
absolute = AB	34–38
appositive = AP	40–43
prepositional = PREP	44–47
participial *(present or past)* = P	48–52
gerund = G	54–57
infinitive = INF	58–62

Clauses	Review These Pages
independent clause = INDC	68–73
adjective clause = ADJC	74–78
adverb clause = ADVC	80–84
noun clause = NC	86–89

PRACTICE 1: IDENTIFYING AND IMITATING THE TOOLS

Model sentences 1–6 illustrate tools listed above. Write the abbreviation for each underlined tool. Next, match the six imitations with the models. Then write your own imitations of models 1–6.

Example:

Sentence: He stood knee-deep (A) <u>in the central grass</u>, (B) <u>looking at his hidden feet</u>, (C) <u>trying to pretend</u> (D) <u>that he was in a tent</u>.

Answers:

(A)—PREP (prepositional phrase)

(C)—P (present participial phrase)

(B)—P (present participial phrase)

(D)—NC (noun clause)

Model Sentences:

1. (A) <u>What they might become in darkness</u> nobody cared to think.

2. (A) <u>Darkish in color</u>, Simon was burned by the sun to a deep tan that glistened with sweat.

3. The densest tangle on the island, (A) <u>a mass of twisted stems</u>, (B) <u>black and green and impenetrable</u>, was on their left.

4. Once more, (A) <u>amid the breeze, the shouting, and the slanting sunlight on the high mountain</u>, was shed that glamour, (B) <u>the strange invisible light of friendship, adventure, and contentment</u>.

5. (A) <u>This boy was now a savage</u>, (B) <u>whose image refused to blend with that ancient picture of a boy in shorts and shirt</u>.

6. There was a speck above the island, (A) <u>a figure dropping swiftly beneath a parachute</u>, (B) <u>a figure that hung with dangling limbs</u>.

Imitation Sentences:

A. The most beautiful bird in the jungle, a flash of bright color, orange and red and striking, was on the banyan tree.

B. That they had to complete this task everyone agreed to accept.

C. This animal was now a pet, whose behavior refused to admit of that other animal in the forest with teeth and claws.

D. Days after, beyond the victory, the celebration and the cheerful backslapping in joyous camaraderie, was felt the great pride, the strong lasting feeling of achievement, success, and esteem.

E. There was a fragrance in the kitchen, a scent wafting deliciously from the oven, a scent that tantalized with spices.

F. Sheepish in embarrassment, Dave was humiliated by the others with some sarcastic remarks that stung with truth.

PRACTICE 2: IDENTIFYING AND IMITATING THE TOOLS

Model sentences 7–12 illustrate tools listed on page 152. Write the abbreviation for each underlined tool. Next, match the six imitations with the models. Then write your own imitations of models 7–12.

Model Sentences:

7. (A) <u>Slowly</u>, (B) <u>toward the end of the afternoon</u>, the mirages were settling a little.

8. The other little boys, (A) <u>whispering</u> but (B) <u>serious</u>, pushed the six-year-old boy toward Ralph.

9. (A) <u>If you could shut your ears to the sound of the sea</u>, (B) <u>if you could forget how unvisited were the ferny coverts</u>, then there was a chance that you might put the beast out of mind and dream for a while.

10. The sand, (A) <u>trembling beneath the heat haze</u>, concealed many figures in its miles of length: (B) <u>boys were making their way along the hot, beach sand</u>.

11. (A) <u>Finally</u>, the laughter died away, and the (B) <u>naming of the boys</u> continued.

12. (A) <u>Two boys set up a pile of brushwood and dead leaves</u>, (B) <u>two dim shadows talking sleepily to each other</u>.

Imitation Sentences:

G. The fog, swirling around the dark trees, hid the branches of the grove of sycamores: limbs were disappearing into the cold white mist.

H. A timid girl approached with a mixture of shyness and quiet determination, a little girl walking hesitantly toward her teacher.

I. The lone heroic student, trembling but courageous, defended his friend without hesitation.

J. When you would remember the rhythm of the surf, when you would recall how the sand felt between your toes, then there was the likelihood that you would escape the winter around you and relax for a moment.

K. Gradually, the sun came out, and the warming of the plants began.

L. Finally, after the joke from the driver, the passengers were laughing a lot.

PRACTICE 3: IDENTIFYING AND IMITATING THE TOOLS

Model sentences 13–18 illustrate tools listed on page 152. Write the abbreviation for each underlined tool. Next, match the six imitations with the models. Then write your own imitations of models 13–18.

Writing Like a Pro

Model Sentences:

13. Piggy knelt by Ralph, (A) <u>one hand on the great conch shell</u>, (B) <u>listening</u> and (C) <u>interpreting to the assembly</u>.

14. Percival, (A) <u>the smallest boy on the island</u>, was mouse-colored and had not been very attractive even to his mother; Johnny, (B) <u>his brother</u>, was well built, (C) <u>with fair hair and a natural belligerence</u>.

15. Ralph would like (A) <u>to have a pair of scissors</u> and (B) <u>to cut his hair</u>—he flung the mass of hair back from his forehead—and cut his filthy hair right back to half an inch, and a bath, (C) <u>a proper wallow with soap</u>.

16. Ralph was down, (A) <u>rolling over and over in the warm sand</u>, (B) <u>crouching with arm to ward off</u>, (C) <u>trying to cry for mercy</u>.

17. Jack stood there, (A) <u>streaming with sweat</u>, (B) <u>streaked with brown earth</u>, (C) <u>stained by all the vicissitudes of the day's hunting</u>.

18. (A) <u>Cautiously</u>, (B) <u>his stick trailing behind him</u>, (C) <u>Ralph wormed between the rising stems</u>.

Imitation Sentences:

M. Jones was mechanical, punching again and again like a robot, aiming with fists to hurt deeply, hoping to end with the championship.

N. Ramona, the unruliest member of the class, was pink-faced, and had not been very attentive even to her friend; Matilda, her companion, was sweet-tempered, with a wonderful spirit and a genuine kindness.

O. Gently, her arm reaching toward him, Susan's fingers wound around his curly locks.

P. Frank ran to Henry, both feet on the fresh green turf, racing and straining for the goal.

Q Fredericka would like to own a pair of Adidas, and to enter the race—she hated the pair of shoes for the team—and run her fastest mile right around the track in a uniform, a team jersey with her name.

R. Brooks puzzled there, thinking about the testimony, befuddled by conflicting evidence, worried by all the contradictions from the trial's witnesses.

PRACTICE 4: IDENTIFYING AND IMITATING THE TOOLS

Model sentences 19–24 illustrate tools listed on page 152. Write the abbreviation for each underlined tool. Next, match the six imitations with the models. Then write your own imitations of models 19–24.

Model Sentences:

19. The flame, (A) <u>invisible at first in that bright sunlight</u>, (B) <u>enveloped in a small twig</u>, grew, was enriched with color, and reached up to a branch, (C) <u>which exploded with a sharp crack</u>.

20. (A) <u>The time had come for the assembly</u>, and (B) <u>as Ralph walked into the splendors of the sunlight</u>, (C) <u>he went carefully over the points of his speech</u>.

21. (A) <u>When the sun sank</u>, (B) <u>darkness dropped on the island like an extinguisher</u>, and (C) <u>soon the shelters were full of restlessness</u>, (D) <u>under the remote stars</u>.

22. (A) <u>Since there was no response to his gentle voice</u>, (B) <u>to carry it stronger and farther</u>, (C) <u>he must speak louder</u> (D) <u>to rouse those striped creatures from their feasting by the fire</u>.

23. He was clambering, (A) <u>heavily</u>, (B) <u>among the creepers and broken trunks</u>, (C) <u>when a bird flashed upwards</u>, (D) <u>a vision of red and yellow</u>.

24. (A) <u>Ralph hit Jack in the stomach</u>, (B) <u>making him grunt</u>; (C) <u>then they were facing each other again</u>, (D) <u>panting</u> and (E) <u>furious</u>, (F) <u>unnerved by each other's ferocity</u>.

Imitation Sentences:

S. She touched her husband on the arm, capturing his attention; then they were walking out together again, laughing and content, thrilled with each other's company.

T. Since there was no applause for his opening joke, to make it funnier and livelier, he would try harder to entertain this jaded audience with their cocktails in their hands.

U. The sound, quiet at first in that huge warehouse, created a steady rhythm, intensified, was amplified with percussion, and turned into a din, which grew into a disturbing cacophony.

V. He was moving, stealthily, around the traps and photosensitive lights when a siren went off, a sound of alarm and danger.

W. The moment was here for the showdown, and when the sheriff turned toward the robbers of the bank, he shouted suddenly to the cowboys in his posse.

X. When the band started, music filled the room like a vaporizer, and then the audience was alive with rhythm from the pulsating sound.

Partners with Pros
Lord of the Flies
by William Golding and YOU!

Become a partner with a pro to learn from your mentor William Golding, author of *Lord of the Flies*. You learned a lot about his style by reviewing in the preceding activity the kinds of sentence-composing tools he uses in his novel. Use those same tools to write a new episode for the novel. (Many high school students have read *Lord of the Flies*. If you haven't, go online to read a summary.)

Creating an Episode

Pretend you are author William Golding, and your publisher wants you to write an extra episode for *Lord of the Flies*: a new ending for the novel.

In Golding's story, a study of the potential for violence and savagery within human beings, a group of young British school boys is stranded on a desert island after their plane crashes. Alone, without adults, the boys are left to their own resources to survive and to govern themselves. The boys, products of privileged civilization and private schools, eventually form two groups, one led by Ralph, the other by Jack, who become rivals, then enemies, and finally leaders of savage tribes, using sharpened sticks for spears to attack each other. In one terrifying incident, Ralph, hiding in a thicket, hears a nearby noise, the sound of the enemy.

Ralph took no time to consider but grabbed his sharp stick and wriggled back among the ferns. Within seconds he was worming his way into the thicket, but not before he had glimpsed the legs of a savage from Jack's tribe coming toward him. Ralph crouched still, tangled in the ferns. He picked up his stick and prepared for battle. Anyone who wormed his way into the thicket would be helpless. He felt the point of his spear with his thumb and grinned without amusement. Whoever tried that would be stuck, squealing like a pig.

Suddenly the branches were shaken furiously at two places on his right. The pointed end of a stick appeared. In panic, Ralph thrust his own stick through the crack and struck with all his might. His spear twisted a little in his hands and then he withdrew it. Someone was moaning outside.

At the end of the story, before the regression becomes complete and the tribes of children destroy each other, they are rescued by a ship and returned to England

and civilization. In retrospect, the horror of their savagery penetrates Ralph's consciousness and he cries uncontrollably:

> The tears began to flow, and sobs shook him. He gave himself up to them now for the first time on the island: great, shuddering spasms of grief that seemed to wrench his whole body. The other little boys began to shake and sob, too. And in the middle of them, with filthy body, matted hair, and unwiped nose, Ralph wept for the end of innocence, the darkness of man's heart.

The novel ends there. But readers question if they are also rescued from their own hearts of darkness and what the future holds for them, especially for Ralph and Jack, the leaders of the savage tribes.

In a new ending for the novel, write an episode that hints at the answer to that question. In several paragraphs, describe a meeting in the future between Ralph and Jack.

Prewriting the Episode

The episode is set someplace in England, twenty years after the ending of the novel when all the young boys were rescued and returned home to England. For the first time since their rescue, Ralph and Jack, now adults, meet. Answer the questions below in a way that will help you plan your episode.

Setting:

1. Where does the meeting take place? How do Ralph and Jack happen to be there?

Characterization:

2. What is Ralph's job and social status?

3. What is Jack's job and social status?

4. What primary aspect of Ralph's personality are you going to emphasize?

5. What primary aspect of Jack's personality are you going to emphasize?

6. What does Ralph look like, and how is he dressed?

7. What does Jack look like, and how is he dressed?

8. In what ways are they happy with their lives? In what ways are they unhappy?

Conflict:

9. In what ways has Ralph changed in twenty years, and in what ways has he remained the same? How is he different from Jack?

10. In what ways has Jack changed in twenty years, and in what ways has he remained the same? How is he different from Ralph?

Theme:

11. What is the main point or theme you want your readers to understand through your episode?

Title:

12. What are some possible titles for your episode?

Drafting the Episode

The following paragraph, written to resemble Golding's style, is the first paragraph of your episode. Copy it. The parts in **boldface** are tools from the list on page 152. See how many you can recognize.

Then continue the episode for several paragraphs, matching the quality of the opening paragraph by using similar tone, vocabulary, and variety of sentence-composing tools to make the episode good enough to appear as the new ending of *Lord of the Flies.*

(1) **Although they had left the island twenty years ago, when the naval officer's cutter had saved them,** the island had never left their memory, **flies buzzing around the pig's hideously decomposing head, haunting all of them, but especially Ralph and Jack, with its recriminations of guilt, shame, and sudden, fierce, naked awareness of the universal potential for evil.** (2) The Lord of the Flies, **which outwardly was a pig's head on a stake,** had become for Ralph and Jack an internal voice of memory and of conscience, **a reminder of their own savagery, intruding into their subsequent lives its relentless horror of spears, of painted faces, of beasts within the darkness of jungle nights and within themselves, and of blood and death by violence.** (3) **What they would never forget from their lost days on the island** had persisted over twenty years, **immutably, indestructibly, like immovable mountains.** (4) Now, **after twenty years of restless lives, their bodies no longer those of boys but of men, their minds still tainted with remnants of childhood's fall from**

innocence, they looked at each other once again, **guiltily, as the horror re-turned in memory**; they listened to each other, **cautiously,** but heard nothing except the echoing voice of the Lord of the Flies, **a voice that they then only dimly but now unmistakably realized was their own.** (5) **Hearing that horrible voice now** silenced their present voices abruptly. (6) **Nervous and somber,** Ralph and Jack finally had their hard reunion, **the first time since the island.** (7) **It was a meeting both men had hoped would never happen,** but **an even more fervent hope required that it would.** (8) This time there was no conch shell—**lost and silent forever**—to symbolize the power of its possessor.

Checklist to Plan, Write, Revise, and Publish Your Episode

☑ Jot down ideas you want to include in your episode. *(prewriting)*

☑ Write a draft of your episode. *(drafting)*

☑ Include the sentence-composing tools your teacher selects from the list on page 152. *(drafting)*

☑ Include examples of the "punctuation of the pros" (semicolons, colons for lists, colons for explanations, and dashes for interruptions) to demonstrate mastery of those special marks. *(drafting)*

☑ Show your draft to students in your class for suggestions. *(peer response)*

☑ Follow good suggestions from peers to revise your episode. *(revising)*

☑ Correct misspellings and errors in grammar and punctuation. *(editing)*

☑ Prepare a neat and attractive final copy for others to read, including your teacher. *(publishing)*

*****

Most great writers agree that good writers are made, not born. They also agree that reading the writing of other writers—like William Golding, Harper Lee, John Steinbeck, Ernest Hemingway, and the hundreds of others in this worktext—is the school where great writers are educated.

Asked her advice for young people who want to write, J. K. Rowling, author of the Harry Potter novels, said, "The most important thing is to read as much as you can, like I did. It will give you an understanding of what makes good writing, and it will enlarge your vocabulary. And it's a lot of fun!"

Read, read, read. Read everything—trash, classics, good and bad, and see how they do it. Just like a carpenter who works as an apprentice and studies the master. Read! You'll absorb it. Then write.

—William Faulkner

In your work in *Grammar for High School: A Sentence-Composing Approach*, you have been a carpenter of sentences, apprenticed to the masters, reading, studying, analyzing, and imitating the ways hundreds of the best writers of our time use grammatical tools to compose their sentences. Those hundreds of writers, your mentors, have taught you how to build better sentences.

Whenever we read a sentence and like it, we unconsciously store it away in our model-chamber; and it goes with the myriad of its fellows, to the building, brick by brick, of the eventual edifice which we call our style.

—Mark Twain

Like a building rising brick by brick, writing unfolds one sentence at a time. The quality of sentences and the grammatical tools they contain largely determine the quality of writing. In his book titled *On Writing,* Stephen King said, "Try to remember that grammar is for the world as well as for school."

In *Grammar for High School: A Sentence-Composing Approach*, you've studied the grammar of the greats to learn the tools our best writers use for building their sentences.

In your school and in your world, make those tools your own, and use them to build better sentences—and a better world.

More help for high school writers from the Killgallons

Sentence Composing for High School
A Worktext on Sentence Variety and Maturity
Don Killgallon

The sentence-composing approach has changed the way thousands of high school English teachers and their students look at language, literature, and writing. **Sentence Composing for High School** presents the same proven methodology but offers all-new writing exercises for high school students.

Unlike traditional grammar books that emphasize sentence analysis, it asks students to imitate the sentence styles of professional writers, making the sentence composing process enjoyable and challenging. **Sentence Composing for High School** offers extensive practice of four sentence-manipulating techniques: sentence unscrambling, sentence imitating, sentence combining, and sentence expanding. Teaching subliminally, nontechnically, it shows students the ways real writers compose their sentences, and helps them intuit new structures within their own writing.

Sentence Composing works anywhere—in any school, with any student. Try it and see your students write with greater variety and maturity.

1998 / 160pp / $20.00
978-0-86709-428-2 / 0-86709-428-1

www.heinemann.com

To place an order, **call 800.225.5800,** or **fax 877.231.6980**

And just for middle school writers . . .

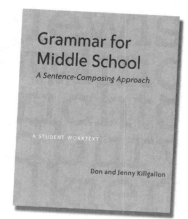

Grammar for Middle School
A Sentence-Composing Approach
A STUDENT WORKTEXT
Don and Jenny Killgallon

In ***Grammar for Middle School: A Sentence-Composing Approach*** the Killgallons use their highly effective method to help students absorb and replicate the grammar used by some of our best prose novelists. Fourteen grammatical structures are developed using sentence-composing activities, and an end-of-section creative writing activity immerses students in the use of the tools they have learned.

Discover how powerful the sentence-composing approach can be, and watch as students get grammar like never before—and write better sentences too.

2006 / 120pp / $12.00
978-0-325-00956-8 / 0-325-00956-2

Sentence Composing for Middle School
A Worktext on Sentence Variety and Maturity
Don Killgallon

Sentence Composing for Middle School presents a powerful, effective way to build sophistication in your writers. It mentors students to professional writers, offering extensive practice of sentence-composing techniques that show students the way authors write sentences and help them work new structures into their own writing.

1997 / 144pp / $20.00
978-0-86709-419-0 / 0-86709-419-2

www.heinemann.com

To place an order, **call 800.225.5800**, or **fax 877.231.6980**